THE SPIRIT OF

PYTHON

D0026988

THE SPIRIT OF
PYTHON

JENTEZEN FRANKLIN

CHARISMA
HOUSE

Most CHARISMA HOUSE BOOK GROUP products are available at special quantity discounts for bulk purchase for sales promotions, premiums, fund-raising, and educational needs. For details, write Charisma House Book Group, 600 Rinehart Road, Lake Mary, Florida 32746, or telephone (407) 333-0600.

THE SPIRIT OF PYTHON by Jentezen Franklin
Published by Charisma House
Charisma Media/Charisma House Book Group
600 Rinehart Road
Lake Mary, Florida 32746
www.charismahouse.com

This book or parts thereof may not be reproduced in any form, stored in a retrieval system, or transmitted in any form by any means—electronic, mechanical, photocopy, recording, or otherwise—without prior written permission of the publisher, except as provided by United States of America copyright law.

Unless otherwise noted, all Scripture quotations are from the New King James Version of the Bible. Copyright © 1979, 1980, 1982 by Thomas Nelson, Inc., publishers. Used by permission.

Scripture quotations marked AMP are from the Amplified Bible. Old Testament copyright © 1965, 1987 by the Zondervan Corporation. The Amplified New Testament copyright © 1954, 1958, 1987 by the Lockman Foundation. Used by permission.

Scripture quotations marked ESV are from the Holy Bible, English Standard Version. Copyright © 2001 by Crossway Bibles, a division of Good News Publishers. Used by permission.

Scripture quotations marked KJV are from the King James Version of the Bible. Public domain.

Scripture quotations marked NAS are from the New American Standard Bible, copyright © 1960, 1962, 1963, 1968, 1971, 1972, 1973, 1975, 1977, 1995 by The Lockman Foundation. Used by permission. (www.Lockman.org)

Scripture quotations marked NIV are from the Holy Bible, New International Version. Copyright © 1973, 1978, 1984, International Bible Society. Used by permission.

Scripture quotations marked NLT are from the Holy Bible, New Living Translation, copyright © 1996, 2004, 2007. Used by permission of Tyndale House Publishers, Inc., Wheaton, IL 60189. All rights reserved.

Scripture quotations marked YLT are from Young's Literal Translation of the Bible. Public domain.

AUTHOR'S NOTE: Some names of persons mentioned in this book have been changed to protect privacy; any similarity between individuals described in this book to individuals known to readers is purely coincidental.

Copyright © 2013 by Jentezen Franklin
All rights reserved

Cover design by Justin Evans
Design Director: Bill Johnson

Visit the author's website at www.jentezenfranklin.org.

Library of Congress Cataloging-in-Publication Data:
An application to register this book for cataloging has been submitted to the Library of Congress.
International Standard Book Number: 978-1-62136-220-3
E-book ISBN: 978-1-62136-221-0

While the author has made every effort to provide accurate telephone numbers and Internet addresses at the time of publication, neither the publisher nor the author assumes any responsibility for errors or for changes that occur after publication.

First edition

13 14 15 16 17 — 9 8 7 6 5 4 3 2 1
Printed in the United States of America

I dedicate this book to my wife, Cherise, and my children—Courteney, Caressa, Caroline, Connar, and Drake. Always keep breathing in the breath of God!

CONTENTS

ACKNOWLEDGMENTS

- To my assistant, Natasha Phillips: thank you for your time, devotion, and dedication. You made it happen again!

- To Debbie Marrie: thank you so much for your brilliant contribution in conveying the thoughts and the teachings contained in this book.

- To Tomi Kaiser: thank you for all your research and hard work on this project; it wouldn't have been possible without you.

- To all the team at Charisma House: thank you for your continued support.

- To the Free Chapel congregation and Kingdom Connection partners: thank you for your prayers and support in all of our endeavors around the world!

INTRODUCTION

ARE YOU FIGHTING internal battles that seem to be getting the best of you?

Maybe your prayer life is not what it used to be, and you just cannot find that place with God that is full of life, joy, peace, and purpose.

You feel as if something has crept in, slowly but surely, and stolen your zeal for praising and worshipping God, to the point that there just doesn't seem to be any time for it anymore. Do you feel limited, hindered, stifled, and unproductive? The battles you are fighting are taking place in the unseen world, where even your close family does not understand what is happening within you. Desires that were once passionate in your heart now seem totally out of reach. Dreams and plans for the future seem to have dried up; the life that was in them has been choked out by something you cannot quite put your finger on.

You and I have a real enemy that battles for the souls of men. He is getting the upper hand in many lives—but we do not have to sit back and let him have access to our homes, our families, or our lives. The Lord has given us power over the enemy; we just need to understand how to use it.

I want to share with you some powerful insights the Lord has given me for overcoming the attacks of the enemy and walking in victory. This book, *The Spirit of Python*, talks about the devil's plan to slowly but surely snake his way into our lives, attempting to choke the very life out of us. I'll help you identify the effects of this subtle but deadly choke hold in your spiritual walk and give you the tools you need to break free and live a victorious Christian life.

From its very opening pages the Bible describes Satan as a snake in the Garden of Eden. Perhaps that's why it's so easy to think of snakes when we think about the devil and his demons. Many years ago I believe the Lord showed me that the devil operates a lot like a snake, a python to be specific, in the way he tries to infiltrate the lives of believers. As he slowly coils his way around us, we hardly even notice—until suddenly we find we can't breathe.

I've preached on this many times, and I have even shared the stage with a live python while doing so in order to get this powerful message into people's hearts. Our enemy is dangerous. He's not playing around. He has one agenda: to steal, kill, and destroy those of us trying to accomplish God's plan. And he knows that if we're not diligent, he can creep in slowly through access we've granted to him, paralyze our ability to pray and worship God, and eventually choke out our spiritual lives altogether.

But there is a way to defeat him! You don't have to become his prey. You can learn to recognize the early warning signs of his deadly grip, discover the ways you may have unknowingly given him an open door into your life and home, and make changes that bring God's deliverance and complete restoration into every area of your life.

So let's get started. I believe this book will change your life and help you overcome even the most powerful attacks!

GOD REVEALS
A DEADLY ENEMY

one

A SNAKE IN THE GRASS

GROWING UP IN North Carolina provided a lot of entertainment for a young boy. My family lived in a pretty rough part of town, right next to a junkyard. Every day trucks stirred up dust as they passed our house on their way to collect or dump their loads.

Joe Baker, one of our closest neighbors, had the distinct reputation of being the town drunk. A lot of folks didn't know that Joe was also one of the nicest people you would ever want to meet. He kept a box of some of the prettiest marbles I'd ever seen and could tell some of the funniest stories my buddies and I had ever heard. You could usually find us at his place a few times a week. We'd walk over, draw a circle in the dirt, get a game of marbles going, and listen to his stories.

When he was younger, Joe's family kept a chicken coop in the backyard. They had one hen that was sitting on a nest of three eggs. Two of them finally hatched, but the last one was holding out. The Bakers didn't have a lot, so they were really looking forward to having more laying hens. They had been watching that last egg anxiously.

Joe and his sister were sitting on the porch one evening when they heard a horrible commotion. Running into the henhouse, they discovered a huge black snake had found a way in, scared off the hen, and swallowed her last egg—*whole*! They could actually see the shape of the egg inside the snake as it slithered out of the coop.

They chased that snake around the yard for a while until it finally crawled into a hole and disappeared. That is where most people would have thrown in the hat, but not Joe and his sister. He said, "My sister handed me a shovel, she grabbed a hoe, and we both started digging like crazy until we saw that snake!"

I remember my friends and I sitting there wide-eyed as Joe continued, "I pulled that egg-stealer out of the hole, cut off its head, and got our egg back. I wiped it off as I carried it back to the nest. I told that mama hen to get up a minute, I put the egg back where it belonged and asked her to get back to the business of hatching us another layin' hen."

He may have been known as the town drunk, but in that situation I think Joe had more revelation than a lot of people. He wasn't about to sit back and let a snake steal what belonged to him and his family.

A VERY REAL ENEMY

For the body of Christ, there has never been a more crucial time for us to wake up and run the snakes out of our hen-houses! I am not one to overemphasize the work of the devil. But even Jesus warned us that the devil only comes to steal, kill, and destroy (John 10:10). He called the devil a murderer and the father of lies (John 8:44). In the Book of Revelation John called him an old serpent who deceives the whole world (Rev. 12:9).

We have a very real enemy, and he first showed up in the Garden of Eden in the form of a serpent. Why a snake? What is the connection between Satan and the serpent?

Just as snakes differ in ways they hunt and destroy their prey, so there are different characteristics of evil spirits and the way they operate. There are snakes that are more venomous than others, just as there are demonic spirits that are more powerful than others. Some serpents kill by biting their victims and injecting deadly poison with their fangs.

But there's one serpent that destroys its prey in a different and unique way. The python is a serpent that waits patiently for its prey and at the opportune moment strikes. It sinks its sharp teeth deep into its victim, but its bite is not fatal. It's what happens next that destroys the prey of the python.

A python is after one thing: *breath*. It slowly coils itself around its victim and begins to squeeze the life out, little by little; as its grip gets tighter and tighter, it chokes and suffocates its prey until all the air is expunged from the prey's lungs.

You might be wondering why I think it is so significant that the python's goal is to suffocate the breath out of its victim. Let me explain. Breath, air, and wind are symbols of the Holy Spirit in Scripture. For example, in John 20:22 Jesus breathed on His disciples and said, "Receive the Holy Spirit." In Acts 2 the Holy Spirit came as a mighty rushing wind; in Genesis God breathed the breath of life into Adam, and he became a living soul. God breathed breath into man.

Guess who's trying to choke and suffocate the life out of us? Satan is after one thing; like a python he is trying to extract the breath of the Holy Spirit and His anointing from our lives. Just as a python hates the breath in his prey and will do anything he can to eliminate it, Satan desires to squeeze the Holy Spirit life out of our churches and personal lives.

He wants that breath of life that only comes through the presence and power of the Holy Spirit. Without the power and anointing of the Holy Spirit we cannot do anything with lasting effect. His Word tells us it's not by might or by power, but by His Spirit (Zech. 4:6).

THE PYTHON

In the twenty-first century I believe the primary spiritual force attacking the church and the life of the believer is the same one that the apostle Paul faced:

> And it came to pass in our going on to prayer, a certain maid, having a spirit of Python, did meet us, who brought much employment to her masters by soothsaying.
>
> —ACTS 16:16, YLT

Most translations record that this woman was possessed with the spirit of divination, but in Young's Literal Translation we see another name for this spirit: *Python.* This is the only time the name of an unclean spirit was given in the Book of Acts. Could it be that God wanted us to understand that there is a spirit of Python that wants to coil itself around every church and every believer, squeezing the spiritual life out of us?

Let me take a few paragraphs to share more about pythons. I believe this will illustrate why this is such a befitting name and image for how the enemy operates.

There are many different species of pythons, and most all of them grow to become huge snakes! The Burmese python is only about 18–20 inches long when it hatches. It starts off small enough to hold in one hand, but it continues to grow until fully mature, when it can average 18–20 feet long and weigh 150–200 pounds.

I cringed a little when I read about a captive Burmese python at Serpent Safari Park, named "Baby." Baby is 27 feet long and weighs just over 400 pounds.[1] Can you imagine coming across a 400-pound snake sunning itself in your garden or dining in your henhouse? That little black snake at Joe's swallowed an egg—but a python as large as Baby can swallow a man!

I once saw a photo of a Burmese python in the Florida Everglades that was in the process of swallowing a large alligator. I don't want to be anywhere around a snake that is tough enough to swallow a gator!

I see too many believers letting that "old serpent" coil his way around their lives, choke out what belongs to them, and leisurely enjoy his meal.

Keep in mind that Burmese pythons are not native to the United States. They have been imported from Asia as pets for years. But once they become too difficult to manage as a result of their size or appetite, careless owners dump them in the wild.

The *climate* in the Everglades is ideal for these large reptiles, and park officials believe there may be roughly one hundred thousand free-roaming pythons there now, gobbling up prey, finding breeding partners, and reproducing.[2] *National Geographic* published an article about the corpse of a 17-foot, 164-pound female python found in the Everglades—carrying a record-setting eighty-seven eggs.[3]

AN UNSEEN WORLD

In Acts 16 Paul and Silas were walking to the place of prayer when the spirit of Python interrupted them. I believe the enemy operates in the same way today. He will interrupt your prayer life. He'll try to stop your praise. You'll always encounter the attack of the enemy just before the Lord shows up in your life. I'll explain more of this in chapters to come.

To me this passage in Acts 16 reveals something very important, and it's why I've written this book. I believe the enemy operates like a python. I'm not talking about the spirit of divination; I'm talking about a strategy of the enemy that works in the very same way that a python attacks its prey. I see too many believers letting that "old serpent" coil his way around their lives, choke out what belongs to them, and leisurely enjoy his meal. I see Christians being overcome instead of overcoming.

Do you feel as if you are losing your passion for the Lord, for the Word, for prayer, and for praise? Don't brush it off as a spiritual slump. Understand that this is the python tactic of the enemy. Are you facing battle after battle, problem after problem, in your home, your marriage, your family, your finances, or your job? Begin to recognize this as the work of the python.

> If Satan can't stop you from receiving Christ
> as your Savior then hell has a "Plan B:" to
> make you a miserable Christian.

The good news is that you have the power to defeat him, and this book contains some deep spiritual insights I believe the Lord gave to me to help you understand and defeat the python-like strategies of the devil.

I'll help you learn more about the key weapons in your spiritual arsenal: prayer, praise, and your spiritual armor. You see, just a few verses later, in Acts 16:25, we find Paul and Silas at midnight, singing praises after they were arrested and beaten for challenging the woman who was possessed with the spirit of Python.

Midnight in Scripture is always a type of the coming of the Lord or the last days. Python tried to stop Paul and Silas just before God showed up in their lives (at midnight). Their story in Acts 16 reveals a lot about why prayer, praise, and the power and presence of the Holy Spirit are vital to your spiritual life— and why these are the very things the enemy seeks to choke out of you. I'll go into greater detail about these in upcoming chapters.

In this book I'm going to offer you some insight into the unseen world of spiritual warfare. The battle between light and darkness is very real. If Satan can't stop you from receiving Christ as your Savior, then hell has a "Plan B:" to make you a miserable Christian. He does this by slowly using the temptations, cares, pressures, and burdens of life to squeeze the joy out of your walk with the Lord.

It's vital that you recognize when the old serpent, that snake in the grass we call the devil, tries to coil himself around you and squeeze the life out of you. Read on to recognize the signs that you are under the attack of the python.

two

ARE YOU UNDER ATTACK?

T HERE WAS A time when someone suffering from a heart attack had little chance of survival because he or she didn't know what was happening and ignored the symptoms until it was too late. Medical advancements began identifying common warning signs such as discomfort and pressure in the center of the chest, pain in one or both arms, and shortness of breath. Spreading awareness of the warning signs has greatly increased the survival rate for heart attack victims.

In a similar manner, many Christians seem to be blindsided by spiritual attacks. When it comes to a spiritual attack, it is crucial to recognize the warning signs for survival.

RECOGNIZE THE SIGNS

Loss of spiritual desire

The goal of any spiritual attack is to turn you away from what God wants to do in your life. That is why the first warning sign of attack is a loss of spiritual desire. We don't live by feelings alone, but there is a difference between doing something merely out of obligation and doing something because you delight in it.

Spiritual desire is evidenced by a heart on fire for God. As David said, "O God, You are my God; early will I seek You; my soul thirsts for You; my flesh longs for You in a dry and thirsty land where there is no water" (Ps. 63:1). When you delight in the Lord, nothing else compares. Someone passionate for God finds pleasure in the things of God.

Losing your spiritual desire rarely happens deliberately. It doesn't take place overnight. It happens slowly—just as the python slowly, methodically begins to tighten his hold on its prey to choke the breath out—and the changes in your heart are subtle. Life issues arise and begin cutting into your time in the Word.

Before long you are just too busy to read your Bible and renew your mind. You start feeling a disconnect when you pray, and before you know it, you start spending less and less time in prayer. Soon you find reasons not to be in church. Worldly pursuits start taking the place of your pursuit of God. Instead of your heart being on fire, it becomes merely lukewarm.

You should have things you enjoy outside of the church—hobbies, skills, sports, activities, travel, and so forth. But I have watched many Christians who were at one time passionate for the things of God begin finding all of their enjoyment in worldly things rather than the things of God.

Physical fatigue

The second warning sign is physical fatigue. I know that doesn't sound very spiritual, but keep in mind that we are created beings—spirit, soul, and body. If my body is weak, it allows things to get into my mind (soul), and that allows things to negatively affect my spirit.

A good example from Scripture is Elijah after his run-in with Jezebel. After having fire fall from heaven and consume his offering, and then killing 850 of her prophets of Baal and Asherah, he delivered a sound blow to her kingdom. That had to be tiring work. Physically exhausting.

That is when Jezebel attacked, sending her messenger to Elijah with her threat to kill him within twenty-four hours. Already worn down, he fled, traveling a full day into the wilderness. When the adrenaline finally wore off, he sat down under a tree and prayed that he would die (1 Kings 19:1–4). Then he fell asleep.

Many times we face our greatest attacks just before a great promotion or just after a great victory. Keep that in mind when you're going through it—an attack could very well be an indication that you are about to be promoted or just had a great victory.

After that tremendous victory, fatigue left Elijah open for attack and feeling like a failure. Fatigue in your body wears on your mind. Your thoughts get twisted—even thinking of suicide. Elijah told God he wanted to die. After he rested awhile, an angel of the Lord awakened him and fed him.

"Lack attack"

The third sign that you are under attack is a "lack attack." There are times when it seems that all of your resources dry up at the same time. Don't get me wrong, I am not implying that Master Card and Visa are demons. You cannot simply "rebuke" debts you have incurred. You can't *pray* bills away; you have to *pay* them. But when everything starts breaking down at the same time, when business dries up or layoffs are announced, the car breaks down, the appliances are on the fritz, and all the kids are sick, you could be under a lack attack. The enemy attacks in this way to get you to take your eyes off of God and put your eyes on money. If he can get you worrying rather than worshipping, you will start making decisions based on opportunity rather than anointing.

I have seen people who were fully committed to God and

growing spiritually and then the enemy hit them with a lack attack. They got their eyes off of God and onto money. Then along came an opportunity—but not an anointed opportunity.

Not every "good" offer is from God. The devil can make some very tempting offers. He even tried to sway Jesus from His purpose, offering Him all the kingdoms of the world and a way out of the cross. Of course, there was a catch. The devil added, "All these things I will give You if You will fall down and worship me" (Matt. 4:9). Your enemy can orchestrate circumstances to give you what you are looking for at a vulnerable moment in your life and steal from you what matters most.

Always remember there are two times in your life when you are especially vulnerable to temptation: when you have *nothing* and when you have *everything*. Stay close to God in both the good times and the bad times. Whether you are in a season when things are going good or a season when nothing is going right, God has promised to supply all of your needs according to His riches in glory as you seek Him first and honor Him with your finances.

If you are going through a lack attack and have more month than you have money, focus your mind on God's promises, not your problems. Remember scriptures like:

> I have been young, and now am old;
> Yet I have not seen the righteous forsaken,
> Nor his descendants begging bread.
>
> —PSALM 37:25

> This Book of the Law shall not depart from your mouth, but you shall meditate in it day and night, that you may observe to do according to all that is written

in it. For then you will make your way prosperous, and then you will have good success.

—JOSHUA 1:8

Does the financial solution pull you away from God's house on Sunday? Does it take you away from your family? We are training a generation to take their life direction from money rather than trusting God. If young people want to work, that is great. But the job needs to allow them to go to church. Never let your kids trade the things of God for minimum wage. The new phone, better car, or cooler jeans are just not worth that much in light of eternity.

> Always remember there are two times in your life when you are especially vulnerable to temptation: when you have *nothing* and when you have *everything*.

One final note before I move on: let me strongly suggest that you make your decisions about tithing *before* a lack attack hits. Tithing is an act of trusting God to take care of the rest. When things get tight financially, it can be difficult to decide whether to pay a bill or honor God with the tithe. Take it to the Lord in prayer, trust Him, and follow His leading.

Weak prayer life

The fourth sign that you are under a spiritual attack is a weakening prayer life. "Could you not watch with Me one hour?" Jesus asked His disciples. Then He told them, "Watch and pray, lest you enter into temptation. The spirit indeed is willing, but the flesh is weak" (Matt. 26:40–41). Hours later Peter found himself under attack, and he denied that he even knew the Lord. The temptation came. The flesh was weak.

Prayer is a discipline. There is no "gift of prayer." It takes action on your part. It takes faith and persistence. However, there are times when even though you are faithful to pray, your mind may work against you.

I often go out in the woods to walk and pray and focus my thoughts on the Lord. But sometimes after walking two or three miles, I realize my thoughts have been on everything *but* God. The enemy wants to circumvent God's will. You'll think of hundreds of things you need to do the moment you try to go pray.

I've learned to take a pen and small notepad with me. After I've written down all the things I've forgotten to do, I say, "Thank you, devil, for reminding me of all these things, and now that that's taken care of, I'm going to pray."

In every failure of my life there have always been two common denominators: a dusty Bible and a broken-down altar. The python strategy of Satan is to squeeze prayer and Bible reading out of your daily agenda.

Remember it's not only the normal or natural duties and cares of life that keep you from your place of prayer and time of prayer; it is an unseen spiritual tactic of the python to choke prayer out of your life. If you are not reading your Bible on a regular basis and praying, you are under spiritual attack. The spirit of Python in Acts 16 attacked Paul and Silas as they went to the temple at their time of prayer (v. 16).

The key to spiritual life is to inhale the Word of God and exhale with prayer. You have a spiritual life if you read the Bible (inhale) and pray (exhale). The Bible is the inspired Word of God, which means it is "God-breathed." So when you read the Bible, you breathe in your spiritual life. When you pray, you exhale. You can't just breathe in; you must also breathe out.

Feeling overwhelmed and hopeless

Are you feeling overwhelmed by circumstances? That could be a sign that you are under attack. The word *circumstance* comes from two words: *circum* (encircle) and *stance* (stand). In other words, you are standing encircled by what's going on. When circumstances feel overwhelming, everywhere you turn there is another problem, and another problem, and another problem. It is as if there is no escape; your problems line up as far as the eye can see and overwhelm you.

In every failure of my life there have always been two common denominators: a dusty Bible and a broken-down altar.

This is one of the tricks the enemy uses to plant the seeds of a bad attitude. Thoughts such as "What's the use? Why even try? Nothing is changing" begin to flood your mind. Frustration takes hold. I read somewhere that frustration is fear that your efforts will not pay off.

It doesn't take long for feelings of being overwhelmed to lead to hopelessness. You just feel like giving up. I want you to understand something about hopelessness. It does not come on all at once. When you hit that wall and just feel like throwing in the towel and quitting—that thought formed in your spirit long before. If quitting is *never* an option, then you will not want to quit when times get hard. You will want to keep pressing on in faith that God's strength is greater than yours and He will see you through every battle.

If you are thinking about quitting, about walking away from

the family of faith, then you are under attack. Remember the python suffocates its victims slowly. Gradually, little by little, the freedom to live is squeezed out of its prey. The Bible says, "Hope deferred makes the heart sick" (Prov. 13:12). It also tells us, "Faith is the substance of things hoped for, the evidence of things not seen" (Heb. 11:1). If the enemy can get you to lose hope, he can get you to stop living by faith.

Old habits and lifestyle resurface

The sixth sign that you are under spiritual attack is that old iniquities begin to resurface in your life. What is an iniquity? Some consider iniquities to be those old habits that your soul wants to fall back on when things don't seem to be going your way—things like smoking, drug abuse, excessive drinking, visiting the bars or clubs, indulging the flesh.

> The key to spiritual life is to inhale the Word of God and exhale with prayer. You have a spiritual life if you read the Bible (inhale) and pray (exhale).

Iniquities also have to do with wickedness and injustice, like lying, cheating, and stealing from others. They include sexual sins such as fornication (sleeping with people to whom you are not married), pornography, and adultery.

Often this sign of attack begins with a longing for your former lifestyle. Perhaps you have thought, "Well, at least when I was in the world, I had this or did that." Like the Israelites complaining in the wilderness, you have selective memory if you are thinking this way.

When Moses led the people of Israel out of Egyptian slavery, every time they encountered a little hardship they complained and wanted to go back—*to slavery!* After a miraculous deliverance out of Egypt, across the Red Sea, and into safety, they got a little hungry and the complaints started rolling out. "Oh, that we had died by the hand of the LORD in the land of Egypt, when we sat by the pots of meat and when we ate bread to the full! For you have brought us out into this wilderness to kill this whole assembly with hunger" (Exod. 16:3).

The children of God still fall into the same patterns today. If you start going back to old iniquities that God has set you free from, if you even start thinking about these things, do not ignore the warning conviction of the Holy Spirit. It is a sure sign that you are under attack, and the lies of the python are coiling around you to pull you under.

Pulling away from godly relationships

When old iniquities start tempting you, the next sign of spiritual attack is sure to follow: pulling away from godly relationships. There was a time when you were in services every time the doors opened. You were among the last to leave the building because you enjoyed talking to and being around other believers.

Look around. Have you pulled out of relationships with people at church or with people in your small group? Are more and more of your friends carnally minded rather than spiritually minded? If so, you are stumbling around on the battleground and the enemy has a target drawn on your head.

When your life is full of God and filled with His Spirit, your unsaved friends will be drawn to Him. Your friends are a photograph of your future. If you have more in common with people in the world than you do with people who serve Christ, you are not connected to the right people.

Mark Your Tree

I remember a time when I was going through a lot of challenges in one particular season. It felt like the darkest valley of my ministry, and I just didn't think I could take anymore. I was under attack. I took a walk in the woods to pray, and I came to a massive oak tree that I often prayed under. As I stood there meditating and praying, crying out to God, I picked up a rock and started carving a mark in the oak tree.

After hitting it a few times, I had cut through the bark and made a permanent mark on it. I said, "God, do You see this mark right here? I don't understand everything that I'm going through right now. I don't know why it is happening. But I do know that You will give me victory in this fight, and the mark on this tree will be a lasting reminder."

> Your friends are a photograph of your future. If you have more in common with people in the world than you do with people who serve Christ, you are not connected to the right people.

Then I said, "Satan, I want you to see this mark too, because I'm never going to give up. I am not going down without a fight. I am never going to stop. I am going to keep going after God harder than ever because this attack must mean that you sense something good is about to break loose in my life."

Since that day I have had many opportunities to look at that mark and confidently reflect on how God brought me through and gave me the victory in that situation. It reminds me that He is faithful, and He *will* do it again.

Do you need to mark a tree in your life? Are you in the midst of a spiritual attack and just can't imagine how you will overcome? Sometimes the battles we face last for days; others last for months and even years. They will try your sanity, but you have to take hold of the promises of God and stand strong in the faith. Put on the whole armor of God and say, "Well, here we go!"

You may not have a literal tree to mark as I did, but you can go to your prayer place (I believe you need a regular place of prayer, which I'll talk more about later), armor up, and fill up on the Word of God. If you will take a stand—He will show up. He will make a message out of your mess. Trust Him, and you will walk away with a testimony of victory.

FIVE "DO NOTS" TO BREAK THE ENEMY'S ATTACK

Once you've "marked your tree" and taken a stand against the enemy's attack, there are five "do nots" that you must remember. The first thing to remember is this: *do not forget who made you.* God created you with storms in mind. He designed you to be weatherproof. Let the winds blow; let the storms rage. You are going to make it through in Him. You are His child, and He cares for you. He wants to see you succeed.

The Bible says the righteous will flourish like a palm tree (Ps. 92:12). I've watched footage of hurricanes as they've moved in. The hurricane winds will break massive oak trees like matchsticks, but not palm trees. Palm trees are designed to bend but not break.

The storm may bend you, but it can't break you—especially if it bends you to your knees and Jesus is the center of your life. Just as the palm tree is built and designed to withstand the storm and even bounce back after the storm passes, more resilient than before, so are you! God built you with that storm in mind.

God has given you bounce-back power. In Micah 7:8 the Bible says, "Do not rejoice over me, my enemy; when I fall, I will arise." God has put a bounce in you like a rubber ball. If life has you down, remember: the harder you fall, the higher you bounce back.

Second, *do not forsake the time and place of prayer.* I've learned there are two things that are vital to a successful prayer life: a time of prayer and a place of prayer. For me the right time is in the morning, and the right place is the beautiful country trails in the woods near my home that I've been walking daily for decades now. It is a place I go that says, "God, I am here to be with You."

I've prayed and walked along these trails through all four seasons—in the spring as the plant life blooms, in the summer when the leaves are bright and green, when they are colorful in the fall, and in the winter when many have fallen. Sometimes I'm just in shorts, a shirt, and sneakers; at other times I'm wearing gloves, a heavy coat, and a hat.

There's a real dynamic that begins to take place when you pray consistently in the same place for years—praying, worshipping, and thanking God for His goodness in the times when everything is going great, and also praying through the tough times when the tears are flowing and the burdens and trials of life feel overwhelming.

Your place of prayer may be a room in your house, a quiet field, a spot in the woods—any place that you have consecrated to God as your meeting place with Him. Without a place of prayer, you will be less and less likely to meet with Him on a consistent basis.

When you are going through hardships, when you are fighting battles, when it feels as if all hell is fighting against you—it can feel hard to pray. If you will just go to your place of prayer, even if you don't know what to pray, you can let Him do the talking. Just going to that place of prayer is an act of surrender to God's will for your life. Your physical presence there says, "I want to hear from You, Father. I don't know what to say, what to pray, but I am here."

Sometimes I will go to my place of prayer and just wait on God. If you do not have a place of prayer, create one. You will make it through the attack because God will pour courage into you every time you have a time of prayer in the place of prayer.

I've learned there are two things that are vital to a successful prayer life: a time of prayer and a place of prayer.

Third, *do not forsake the place of power.* When you get into a spiritual battle, the enemy will try to pull you away from church. He'll do it with all of his might. As long as the prodigal son was in the father's house, he was safe; it was when he abandoned the father's house and went into a foreign country that he lost everything.

In Psalm 20 the people prayed for David, "May the LORD answer you in the day of trouble; may the name of the God of Jacob defend you; *may He send you help from the sanctuary,* and strengthen you out of Zion" (vv. 1–2, emphasis added).

Your church is a place of power. Don't forsake the place of power. When the enemy tells you ten reasons to stay home, that's when you should start getting ready to go even faster, knowing that God has a word to strengthen you that you may not hear anywhere else.

Some Christians are tumbleweed Christians, just blowing from church to church. Tumbleweeds are rootless and fruitless, but a tree is planted (Ps. 92:13–14). Be a tree, not a tumbleweed!

Fourth, *do not forsake the power of partnership.* Wise Solomon said, "Two are better than one, because they have a good reward for their labor. For if they fall, one will lift up his companion. But woe to him who is alone when he falls, for he has no one to help him up" (Eccles. 4:9–10).

The enemy's tactic never changes; he wants to divide and conquer. That is how the snake Satan first deceived Eve; he got her alone and twisted the words of God.

But you need to use wisdom in choosing which relationships you should cultivate. "Iron sharpens iron" (Prov. 27:17). You don't need to support toxic, dysfunctional, draining relationships. You need the power of partnership that holy relationships provide. It is good to be around people who have lived longer and done more than you have. You can glean from their experience, including their mistakes.

When you are going through an attack, you don't need deadbeat friends who want to drag you down further. You need to be around spiritual giants who have fought the good fight of faith and are still standing.

Fifth, *do not disconnect from pastoral protection.* God has given pastors the responsibility of feeding and protecting the flock. That is why Hebrews 13:17 says, "Obey those who rule over you, and be submissive, for they watch out for your souls, as those who must give account. Let them do so with joy and not with grief, for that would be unprofitable for you."

The shepherd sees the wolf coming even when you don't know you are under attack. David said of the Lord, the Good Shepherd, "Yea, though I walk through the valley of the shadow of death, I will fear no evil; for You are with me; Your rod and Your staff, they comfort me" (Ps. 23:4). The shepherd's staff had a hook on the end, used for pulling a lamb out of danger. His rod was used as a weapon against predators.

I have often seen people under attack whom I wanted to pull close and help, but they refused. Do not wait until your enemy is tearing you to pieces to seek the aid of those in a pastoral role in your life.

In the next chapter I'll discuss spiritual warfare and the different types of evil spirits doing battle against you and me. The enemy is cunning. He knows how to blindside you and catch you off guard, but as you read on, you will arm yourself against his schemes. You are equipping yourself to fight and win!

three

ATMOSPHERE IS EVERYTHING

DUE TO THE locations of our Free Chapel campuses, I've made many flights from Orange County, California, to Atlanta, Georgia, but one of those flights was unforgettable. That particular flight offered passengers a movie called *Snakes on a Plane*. It's a movie about a cage of deadly venomous snakes that escape and start attacking the passengers. Of course there is nowhere to hide from the snakes when you are flying at forty thousand feet.

Needless to say, it was pretty ironic to be watching a movie like that while on a plane. But even more ironic was that two rows behind me sat the star of the movie, Samuel L. Jackson. I must admit, when we landed I took a picture of him and tweeted about the irony of being on a plane with Samuel L. Jackson while watching *Snakes on a Plane*. Thankfully that battle with snakes was just a movie, but we all face very real battles with spiritual snakes every day.

Scripture teaches that there are spiritual battles taking place all around us because we live in two atmospheres at the same time. One is a physical atmosphere that we can see, smell, hear, touch, and taste. The other is a spiritual atmosphere. We cannot see it with the natural eye or experience it with the rest of our natural senses, but it is very real, and it is vital that we understand more about it.

Have you ever sensed a tightness in the atmosphere? I once watched a television program about prison guards. Many have developed strong instincts from years of experience in working with prisoners. They can tell when a fight is about to break out because they can feel a change in the atmosphere. They have a sense that something is not right. They say there is a tenseness when a fight is about to break out in a federal penitentiary.

Have you ever walked into a room when two people were having an argument? Maybe you didn't see it or hear it, but you could feel tenseness in the atmosphere of that room because of the words that had been spoken and the argument that had taken place moments before you walked in.

Maybe you've gone to a family function where some of the family members have had issues with each other for years. There is tenseness in the atmosphere in a situation like that when the offended parties walk into the room. No words have to be said for you to feel the tension. All it takes is for someone to respond to that atmosphere, and it could wreck the whole family reunion because the atmosphere is so tense.

The devil knows the power of atmosphere. That's why most people are enticed into the wrong atmosphere first before they are ever tempted to sin. The enemy knows that if he can get you in a wild club or party scene, you are much more prone to sin than you are in a library. What's the difference? Atmosphere.

You can grow bananas in Jamaica but not in Alaska. Why? The atmosphere is right for banana growing in Jamaica, but it's not right in Alaska. There's something about the atmosphere of a club—the lights, the music, the dancing—it creates an environment that is right for sin. The atmosphere creates a climate, and the climate creates a culture. If the enemy can get you in his culture, he knows he can get you to sin.

The same is true with the Holy Spirit: atmosphere is everything. The atmosphere of holiness, purity, praise, worship, prayer, love, and unity attract the Holy Spirit—just as an atmosphere of lust, drunkenness, anger, and hatred attracts demonic spirits.

God responds to atmosphere as well. He is everywhere—but He does not manifest His presence equally everywhere. God manifests His presence when the atmosphere is right. He loves a celebration. He loves the atmosphere of praise and of true worship from His people. The Bible says that God inhabits the praises of His people (Ps. 22:3). The word *inhabits* means He is enthroned or feels comfortable enough to sit down in the place where the atmosphere is filled with celebration, praise, and worship. When you fill the atmosphere with complaining, fault-finding, and murmuring, it's not inviting to the presence of God. It has quite the opposite effect.

If you are filled with the Holy Spirit and He is dominating your life, then the fruit of the Spirit—love, joy, peace, long-suffering, kindness, goodness, faithfulness, gentleness, and self-control—will become increasingly evident in your life (Gal. 5:22–23). When the fruit of the Spirit is in your life, you naturally create an atmosphere for the presence of the Holy Spirit. "And in him you too are being built together to become a dwelling in which God lives by his Spirit" (Eph. 2:22, NIV). As you respond to the presence of God, He releases greater measures of His presence.

Have you ever been in a church where you can sense tightness in the atmosphere? We know that our God is our healer, so why do some churches never see any physical healings take place? There are no healings because there is no atmosphere for miracles. There is a limited atmosphere of faith.

The lack of faith in the atmosphere can limit what we see God do in our midst. When Jesus was ministering in His hometown of Nazareth, because of their unbelief He couldn't perform many miracles there except for healing a few sick people (Mark 6:5–6).

Miracles happen when the atmosphere is right. When people begin to respond to the presence of God, He responds to the people in greater measure. That is why some people receive healing or supernatural deliverance from addictions during a powerful worship service, or why sometimes, before the altar call is ever given, unsaved people will get out of their seats, weeping and walking to the front to repent and ask Jesus into their lives—because the atmosphere is so charged with the presence of God. The atmosphere is so holy that sinners can't stand it any longer, and they fall under such conviction that they are compelled to come forward. That is the kind of atmosphere I love to be in!

What kind of atmosphere does your life have? Are you attracting the Holy Spirit, or is the atmosphere just right for a demonic invasion?

DIFFERENT TYPES OF DEMONS

Demonic spirits with different ranks and assignments exist in the spiritual realm. They also respond to atmospheres. All spirits seek expression of their will into time and space, but they can't accomplish this without somebody providing them the opportunity. If a demonic spirit is going to manifest, it will happen because somebody allowed it and created an atmosphere for it.

You are at war, but you cannot fight in the spirit realm with your natural ability, education, money, or natural resources.

You have to fight spirit with spirit, "For the weapons of our warfare are not carnal but mighty in God for pulling down strongholds" (2 Cor. 10:4).

When the disciples asked Jesus why they were unable to cast the evil spirit out of the child, Jesus said, "This kind does not go out except by prayer and fasting" (Matt. 17:21). "This kind" would indicate that there are spirits with different ranks.

Without going into an expository work on demonology, in general there are a few different types of evil spirits mentioned in the Bible. Allow me to give you a brief explanation of them.

Tormenting or vexing spirits

A tormenting or vexing spirit is a lower-ranking demon that comes to oppose your mind and bring depression, fear, and excessive worry. Having a bad day is not necessarily an indication that you are being tormented by a demon. Real life can get difficult. But when you feel oppressed all the time, that you are in a rut where your mind and emotions are in turmoil, you are down, depressed, discouraged, and feeling hopeless—that is a different story.

The enemy whispers suggestions for you to just give up. Maybe thoughts creep in to your mind of harming yourself, or even suicide.* That is a vexing spirit tormenting your mind. Let there be no doubt—as a born-again believer you have been given authority over any demon that tries to torment your life. God gives us "the garment of praise" for the spirit of heaviness or despair (Isa. 61:3).

When a vexing spirit tries to torment you, your first response should be to take authority over it and rebuke it in the name of Jesus. Do not give in to those negative, harmful, demonic

---

* If you have thoughts of harming yourself or others, it's imperative that you seek professional help in addition to following the advice provided in this book.

thoughts of despair. Resist them. If you humble yourself and resist the devil, he *will* flee.

Your second response should be to lift up praise to God because it will change the atmosphere and cause a shift in the spiritual realm. As a Christian, the greatest thing you can do to combat depression and oppression in your mind is to put on the garment of praise. Put on some worship music and transform your heart and mind into an attitude of gratitude. Think on good things.

I tell people to speak "praise phrases" where you verbally praise the Lord. "You are good. You are working all things together for my good." That's how you defeat tormenting spirits of the mind. Remember, atmosphere is everything, so don't give in and begin to say words that make the devil think he's winning. Speak words of praise, and that spirit of heaviness will lift.

Deceiving spirits

The second type of evil spirit has to do with wrong teaching, false teaching, and wrong thought patterns. Paul told Timothy, "Now the Spirit expressly says that in latter times some will depart from the faith, *giving heed to deceiving spirits and doctrines of demons*" (1 Tim. 4:1, emphasis added). This verse tells us there are demons that pervert teachings, twist the Word of God, and lead people away from the faith.

Any time you open yourself up to doctrines of demons and false teachings—including horoscopes, fortune-tellers, palm readers, and psychics—you are opening the door to Satan's plan for your life. You are also getting yourself into spiritual territory that you cannot conquer on your own. Any believer can take authority over a vexing spirit, but only pastors, teachers, evangelists, prophets, and apostles have authority to take the

Word of God and teach truth against doctrines of devils and false teachings. If you or someone you know has opened these doors to the enemy, I encourage you to seek the counsel of your pastor or a mature believer in Christ.

Territorial spirits

There are higher-level territorial principalities that try to control certain geographical areas. Certain cities are known for certain influences, such as Las Vegas with gambling, Los Angeles with entertainment, New York with finance, and Washington DC with politics and power. These territorial spirits are demonic powers trying to control the culture over a city, region, state, or nation.

Any time you open yourself up to horoscopes, fortune-tellers, palm readers, and psychics, you are opening the door to Satan's plan for your life.

It takes a community of believers praying and fasting and establishing strong churches in those cities, regions, and states that deal with the principalities in high places. Jesus said, "I will build My church, and the gates of Hades [hell] shall not prevail against it" (Matt. 16:18). That is what Paul was talking about when he said, "His intent was that now, *through the church*, the manifold wisdom of God should be made known to the rulers and authorities in the heavenly realms" (Eph. 3:10, NIV, emphasis added).

WHAT YOU NEED TO KNOW
ABOUT DEMON POSSESSION

As believers we have been given authority over demons. The only way demons can get a stranglehold on us is when we deliberately and persistently walk in sin. If a believer encounters what he thinks is a true manifestation of demon possession, he has authority and the power of the Holy Spirit to expel that demon power. I believe if someone does encounter someone they suspect is demon possessed, they should call upon a trusted mature believer to aid them and have at least two or three together to pray for guidance in the situation.

What are the signs of demon possession? First, demons are able to energize people with incredible strength. In the case of the man possessed by the demonic spirit, Legion, he had been bound with heavy chains and broke them; no one could subdue him. (See Mark 5.) I have seen a few people who were demon possessed, and sometimes it would take five or six people to subdue them. They displayed more than human strength; they displayed supernatural strength from a demonic power.

A person who is demon possessed may have spontaneous reactions of uncontrolled cursing when the name of Jesus Christ is mentioned. An uncontrolled compulsion to blaspheme the name of God can be a sign of demonic influence. A radical change in personality can also be a telltale sign.

An evil spirit can cause contortions in facial features and countenance, and the eyes can become glazed. The look and even the voice of a demon-possessed person can change. When someone is set free from demon possession, their personality often changes immediately. Their voice will normalize, and you will see a total change in their demeanor.

As I mentioned previously when discussing tormenting and

vexing spirits, deep depression, despondency, and suicidal tendencies can also be signs of demonic attack. These conditions can go beyond spiritual torment to a level that we would consider demonic possession or oppression.*

There are some examples in Scripture of demon-possessed people who tried to harm themselves. After Satan used Judas for his purpose, he then used the power of guilt to drive Judas to self-destruction. Judas hanged himself.

The demon-possessed boy in Matthew 17:14–15 had a strong tendency for self-destruction. He threw himself into the fire and then into the water trying to harm himself. This was the result of the demon's attempt to inflict harm and self-destruction on the child. The demoniac of Gadara gashed himself with sharp stones, indicating how demons arouse a tendency toward self-destruction.

Today many teenage girls cut themselves. This does not necessarily mean they are demon possessed, but certainly the voice telling them to slash themselves or starve themselves with anorexia is not the voice of the Holy Spirit. The bottom line is every case of suicide or of self-destructive acts is different, but when someone is repeatedly trying to harm himself or herself, there is a strong possibility that person could be under demonic attack.

Extreme caution should be used when discerning whether someone is demon possessed or not. In more than twenty-five years of ministry I have only encountered five people whom I was convinced needed some form of exorcism. I have found when attempting to cast out demons, it should almost always

---

* Be careful when weighing any of these symptoms, which can be brought on by other causes such as chemical imbalances or mental illnesses. Seek professional help if you or someone you are trying to help experiences thoughts of self-harm or harming others.

be done in a private setting with a pastor or other mature, balanced spiritual leaders present.

James 4:7 says, "Resist the devil and he will flee from you." This is the position of the born-again believer. Jesus Christ in His ultimate commission to the church said in Mark 16:17, "In My name they will cast out devils." So again, seek the help of a mature Christian leader, but don't be afraid to take authority over demons as a believer in Christ.

Let me share a true story that happened when I was twenty-one years old and was on a twenty-one-day fast. In the second week of that fast, I was preaching a revival in North Carolina with my brother Richie. We had an unusual service one night. The Holy Spirit moved in a powerful way as we began to sing a song. The altars filled with hundreds of people, and many were coming to be saved and filled with the Holy Spirit.

After the service a man dressed in a nice suit asked if he could meet with my brother and me in a private room. He asked if we would please pray for him. As I gently laid my hand on his shoulder and began to pray, suddenly I sensed an unnerving spiritual presence. I knew we were dealing with something that until this time had been only a doctrine I had read about in the Bible. I knew what the Bible had to say about demonic possession, but I had never been called upon to deal with someone who was under the influence of an evil spirit.

What happened in the next twenty minutes was an amazing experience. This man dressed in a nice suit began to change right before our eyes. His countenance changed, his voice began to get deeper, and an evil spirit spoke through this man, "We will not leave. We hate you. Leave us alone."

I was horrified and remember thinking to myself, "If you will not leave, I will! I'm getting out of here!"

Suddenly I felt a boldness and authority from the Holy Spirit that I had never felt before. Something inside of me said, "Greater is He that is in you than he that is in the world. This kind comes out but by fasting and prayer."

I laid my hand on the man and said, "Satan, in the name of Jesus Christ, I command you to loose this man and set him free." He began coughing and gagging. I could literally smell a sulfur-like scent in the room. It was the strangest thing. Even to this day it confounds me.

After I spoke those words, the man's countenance and voice returned to normal, and he began weeping. He asked Jesus to be Lord of his life. He later confessed to my brother and me that he was addicted to pornography and was having an affair with a married woman in the church.

I realize to the skeptic this sounds sensational and dramatic, but the truth is, it really happened, and he was truly set free by the power of God from demonic power.

Let's take a look at a Scripture passage from Isaiah chapter 14. It gives us the key to the origin of evil. When this passage was written, God was mourning over this creature whom He had created and loved.

> How art thou fallen from heaven, O Lucifer, son of the morning! How art thou cut down to the ground, which didst weaken the nations! For thou hast said in thine heart, I will ascend into heaven, I will exalt my throne above the stars of God: I will sit also upon the mount of the congregation, in the sides of the north: I will ascend above the heights of the clouds; I will be like the most High.
>
> —Isaiah 14:12–14, KJV

The creature we call Satan was described first as *Lucifer,* which means "the shining one." He was so beautiful that he would literally shine with the glory of God. But take a look at that passage again. Notice the verse that begins, "For thou hast said *in thine heart...*" This is the description of evil. This is where it all began.

Sin originates in the heart. Five times he said in his heart, "I will." Lucifer filled his heart with rebellion. He wanted to act independently of God. He was saying to God, "Since I am so magnificent, so beautiful, so filled with power, why shouldn't I have some of the worship of the universe for myself?"

Lucifer said, "I will ascend to heaven," In other words, he was saying, "Move over, God, I'm going to be in charge now. I will make myself like the Most High." He wanted to be God.

Apparently a great rebellion erupted throughout the universe at that time. Lucifer led the revolution among the angels. We are told in Revelation 12 that one-third of the angelic realm followed Lucifer in his revolt.

I don't believe Lucifer lost any of his great intellect, beauty, or power when he rebelled and became the first sinful creature. I believe he used these traits to entice many angels to join his ranks. But he did lose the one thing that would make him function correctly: a personal relationship with God.

At that moment God's perfect universe became impure. The pollution of sin entered the earth when Satan and his angels revolted.

Today Lucifer is known by many names and descriptions: Satan, the devil, the evil one, the accuser, the adversary. This little planet known as earth has become the arena of the mightiest contest of all time—a contest between good and evil, a contest between God and Satan, a contest where God

Himself would be wounded in a life-and-death struggle with the powers of darkness.

In the garden God gave the title deed of the world to Satan, and since then the world has been under his control. The Bible gives Satan three titles that describe his work. First, he is called "the ruler of this world" (John 12:31), which means he is constantly at work in government and political systems in nations throughout the world.

Satan's second title is "prince of the power of the air." Ephesians 2:1–2 says, "And you...were dead in trespasses and sins, in which you once walked according to the curse of this world, according to the prince of the power of the air, the spirit who now works in the sons of disobedience."

The word translated as "air" in this scripture literally means "the air we breathe," and it is speaking of "mood" or "atmosphere of thought." We often use the term atmosphere in this sense. For instance, if someone says, "Paris has a romantic atmosphere," you would understand that they were talking about a certain mood or feeling in the air.

So in his letter to the Ephesians, Paul calls Satan the prince of the "atmosphere of thoughts" of this world system that are hostile to God. In this role Satan injects his brainwashing into the educational system, mass media, arts, the style, and culture. His deceptions about life and its purpose are lethal.

Before you believe in Jesus Christ, you are unwittingly dominated by this atmosphere of thought. But when you realize that he is the ruler over all these thought forms and realize the ways in which you are bombarded every day by these sources, you begin to see how deadly the prince of the power of the air can be.

That's why we have to focus our hearts on Jesus and constantly have our minds renewed with God's view of life, which is alien from the human viewpoint of the world's systems. That's why Romans 12:2 says, "And do not be conformed to this world, but be transformed by the renewing of your mind."

Satan's third title is "the god of this age" (2 Cor. 4:4), which means the prevailing thought of a particular era. The god of this age refers to Satan's activity in relation to religion.

ATMOSPHERES, CLIMATES, STRONGHOLDS, AND CULTURES

When you respond to any of the spiritual influences or activities I've just described, you create an atmosphere. The atmosphere you sustain over time will create a climate (a predictable pattern). For example, you might live in an area that has a hot day now and then, but that does not create a hot climate like the one you would experience in a tropical area where temperatures are always balmy. A climate comes from the repetition of the same thing.

Whenever we sustain a spiritual atmosphere of praise and thankfulness, a climate of God's presence begins to form. Conversely, whenever we sustain a spiritual atmosphere of sin and iniquity, a demonic climate takes shape.

If a sustained atmosphere creates a climate, then a climate creates a stronghold. The stronghold defines the culture of a place. Demonic spirits fight for control to define the culture of nations.

The enemy is out to set up a culture that is void of the power of God. Even in the church there is little difference between some Christians' lifestyles and the world's lifestyles. The morals are very much alike and reflective of one another.

Don't Leave Them Alone

Once the enemy gains ground in getting that kind of culture set up, then he wants to be left alone. Luke 4:33–34 tells us that while ministering in Capernaum, Jesus encountered a man in the synagogue who had an unclean demon, and he cried out in a loud voice, "Let us alone!"

Satan and his demons would rather do their work without being exposed. They definitely don't like to be identified and cast out. Demons resist exposure and will resist anyone who attempts to bring the light of God upon their hidden works.

Many well-meaning Christians, including pastors, feel it is not necessary to discuss or teach on spiritual warfare. Anyone who does spend time studying and teaching in these areas of Scripture is considered overboard, radical, or a "demon-chaser."

These ministers of the gospel who don't want to deal with the subject of demons will often say that all they need to do is preach Jesus. I'm certainly not against preaching Jesus, but I also find in Luke 4:18 that we are called to preach deliverance to the captives. Jesus was a deliverance preacher. In Mark 6:13 He cast out many devils. Today most ministries—including mine—cast out few if any.

Demons resist exposure and will resist anyone who attempts to bring the light of God upon their hidden works.

Many don't want to deal with this aspect of the ministry of our Lord. But avoidance of spiritual warfare teaching is just what the enemy wants. The less you discuss and attack the python's kingdom, the more he will be able to operate under the cover of darkness.

Some ministries unconsciously fall into the trap of the enemy by *leaving him alone*. In Mark 1:23–24 there was in the synagogue a man crying out, "Let us alone." The cry of this spirit is the cry of *all* evil spirits: "Let us alone!" They don't like to be disturbed!

If demons are left alone, they will continue to operate unhindered in the lives of countless individuals. That's precisely why demons cannot and should not be left alone; they must be exposed and cast out by the power of God's Word and the Holy Spirit. Just as demons were exposed in Jesus's day and at times they screamed, cursed, and cried out, so they must also be exposed today.

According to Ephesians 6:12, demons are identified as "the rulers of the darkness of this world" (KJV). Rulership denotes authority. In other words, a demon's level of authority to operate is based upon the darkness in a person's life. The more darkness, the more authority they have.

In contrast, when revelation comes from God's Word concerning their works and schemes, then light comes. When light comes, the darkness is dispelled and their power is broken. This is why Satan and his demons would rather be left alone.

Do you know why the Bible says in Mark 6:13 that Jesus and His disciples "cast out many devils"? Because they were there! The Lord is raising up ministries that will not leave demons alone but will expose and defeat them with the power and light of God's truth. We must challenge, confront, and expose the works of darkness. "But through knowledge the righteous will be delivered" (Prov. 11:9).

You see, everything was all right until Jesus entered the temple and cast them out. The religious system of that day had not disturbed them; the preaching and teaching of the

Pharisees and Sadducees did not disturb them. You can't cast the devil out if you're best friends with him. But the teaching and preaching of Jesus infuriated them. He exposed them and defeated them.

In Exodus 14:12 the Hebrews said the same thing to Moses that the demons said to Jesus: *"Let us alone* that we may serve the Egyptians"* (emphasis added). They were being motivated by the spirits of bondage, slavery, and fear to say, "Leave us alone."

It's Time for a Climate Change!

It is important to understand atmospheres and your ability to change them because Jesus has authorized and empowered you to do so. I have heard it said that Christians are not to be spiritual *thermometers* but spiritual *thermostats*. In other words, you are not merely supposed to *detect* the spiritual climate as a thermometer detects the existing temperature in a room; you are to *change* it, imposing the authority of the kingdom of God wherever you go.

You can't cast the devil out if you're best friends with him.

How do you usher in a climate change? Start by changing the atmosphere. Keep a spirit of prayer and praise in your life. It creates the right atmosphere around you.

Jesus changed the atmosphere in His region. You have the power to change the atmosphere and usher the presence and power of God into your situation, your home, and your church. This is how you keep the python out. You must refuse to leave him alone.

Do you have unsaved loved ones who need to hear the message of the gospel but something keeps blocking them from hearing and receiving? Do not back down. Change the atmosphere with prayer and praise. Stand and fight, filled with the Holy Spirit. Go to the throne of God on your knees and intercede for them. It's time to drive the snake out of your life!

Souls are at stake. People we love are bound in sin. Many still stumble in darkness. We have the authority to stand between new converts, our families, our children, and the spirit of this age that wants to pervert the truth of God and turn them away.

That is why we fast, pray, praise, worship, intercede, and stand and wage war in the spiritual realm. This is why we cannot let our enemy, the python, work his way into our lives, squeeze the life out of us, and render us ineffective.

In this chapter I spoke about different spirits and how you invite them into your life and allow them to affect the atmosphere and gain control. In the next chapter I'll explain in more detail the many common ways we open windows and doors to the python in our lives.

four

WHO LET THE SNAKES IN?

THAT SNAKE IN chapter 1 got into Joe's chicken coop by patiently looking until it found a point of access. I'm sure it tried a few different openings, sat back all coiled up as it waited for the opportune moment, until it finally found a way in. Except for a noisy and protective mother hen sounding the alarm, that sneaky, slimy predator would have gotten away with it.

The devil operates in the same way in our lives. But the good news is that once we learn to identify the openings we leave for him, we can get rid of his influence, shut the door on him, and destroy his access to our lives. We don't have to be his prey. We can defeat the python because Jesus has stripped him of all his power.

Writing about Jesus, the author of the Book of Hebrews said that Jesus took on flesh, became like one of us, and defeated the devil (Heb. 2:14). Scripture makes it clear that Jesus stripped the devil of all power and authority through His death, burial, and resurrection: "Having disarmed principalities and powers, He made a public spectacle of them, triumphing over them in it" (Col. 2:15). In Revelation 1:18 the Lord proclaimed that He is the one who was dead but now lives forever and holds the keys of Hades and death.

Now, I want you to think about something for a moment. If

you do not have this revelation already, I believe it will change your life: Jesus has the keys of hell and death, so what keys does Satan still have? None! He doesn't even have the keys to his own kingdom anymore.

Jesus openly subdued him and his minions, and God gave Jesus all rule and authority in this age and the age to come. The kingdom of heaven knows it. The kingdom of darkness knows it. The problem is, too many Christians do not live like they know it, so they are not operating from that position of victory.

I like how the prophet Isaiah described the fall of Lucifer:

> How you are fallen from heaven, O Lucifer, son of the morning! How you are cut down to the ground, you who weakened the nations!...Yet you shall be brought down to Sheol, to the lowest depths of the Pit. Those who see you will gaze at you, and consider you, saying: "Is this the man who made the earth tremble, who shook kingdoms, who made the world as a wilderness and destroyed its cities, who did not open the house of his prisoners?"
>
> —ISAIAH 14:12, 15–17

Isaiah used words like *fallen, cut down,* and *brought down.* In the last verses he describes how shocked people will be when they see Satan in his defeated state—as the small, powerless demon that he is. They will probably need to squint their eyes a little to see him and wonder how he did so much damage. Satan has been defeated, but he still wreaks havoc in the world. Where then does he get his power?

FOOTHOLDS IN OUR LIVES

Giving some "how-to" instruction to the Ephesian church, Paul wrote, "You were taught, with regard to your former way of life, to put off your old self, which is being corrupted by its deceitful desires; to be made new in the attitude of your minds; and to put on the new self, created to be like God in true righteousness and holiness" (Eph. 4:22–24, NIV). Notice three distinct steps there.

If you do not have this revelation already, I believe it will change your life: Jesus has the keys of hell and death, so what keys does Satan still have? None!

First, *put off the old way of life*. Second, *renew your mind and put on your new self*. In talking about the old self, Paul mentions lust, impurity, falsehood, lying, anger, bitterness, stealing, unwholesome talk, rage, brawling, slander and every form of malice. But notice in the midst of that list he states the third step: *"Do not give the devil a foothold"* (v. 27, NIV).

If you have ever been rock climbing or indoor climbing, you know that a foothold doesn't have to be very big. It can be just a little bump, even a small crevice. As long as it is something that you can wedge the edge of your big toe and ball of your foot against, you can use it to push yourself up to higher ground.

The devil looks for footholds in a believer's life because he knows that we have been given the victory in Christ, but when we give way to him and allow a foothold, we give away that victory. All the things Paul associated with your old self will act as footholds for the devil to gain ground, gain access, and gain *power* in your life. They open doors and windows for the python to enter your home and wrap himself around you, your spouse, and your children.

SATAN'S REALM OF INFLUENCE

Man is made of spirit, soul, and body. I hate to break it to you, but no matter how much time you spend at the salon or how often you hit the gym, your physical body will one day stop working and start to decay. Flesh gives birth to flesh that decays, but the Holy Spirit gives birth to the spirit that is eternal.

That is why Jesus explained to Nicodemus that one must be born of water and Spirit in John 3:5–6. While I do believe that disease and illness can be an assignment of the enemy, I believe that in large part we do so much damage to our bodies through our own appetites that the devil doesn't have to make our bodies his main target. Since he cannot touch our spirits, his focus is on our *souls*.

God breathed life into Adam at the creation of the world, making him a living soul. A soul is a uniquely human feature. Unlike any other creation God made, mankind has been given the ability to make choices and decisions. As I mentioned in the previous chapter, you and I make choices every day that affect the spiritual atmosphere and empower the operation of one of two kingdoms: either the kingdom of light or the kingdom of darkness.

Satan's realm of influence is in the human soul—the center of the mind, will, and emotions. The only power the devil has in this world is the power we turn over to him through our choices and actions. When we rebel, when we sin, when we follow our fleshly desires rather than the Holy Spirit, we empower the kingdom of darkness.

Remember the scripture from Isaiah 14 that I shared in the last chapter? Pride was found in Lucifer *before* he was the devil. He said, "I will ascend above the heights of the clouds, I will be like the Most High" (v. 14). Lucifer was a beautifully decorated angel of music. He was in the presence of God before Creation. Ezekiel 28:15 says he was perfect from the day he was created until iniquity was found in him.

You can be a Christian and still be full of pride. It is the subtlest of all sins because it is rooted in self-will. Isaiah said that like sheep we have all gone astray, and each of us has turned to his own way (Isa. 53:6). Notice that he didn't say each has turned to the devil's way, or to the world's way, but rather to *his own* way.

Self-will has to do with following your own way and adhering to your own opinions and desires. For example, many people who claim to be Christians try to conform the Word of God to fit their *lives* rather than conforming their lives to the *Word of God*. The devil, acting like a python, squeezes until they stop reading the Word of God, which is like inhaling spiritual breath. Pretty soon, as the python continues to squeeze, doubts creep in. They believe the Bible about certain things, but not everything. They start thinking they can be a Christian but live the way they want to live instead of following the Bible. That kind of self-will and stubbornness is what the Bible calls idolatry (1 Sam. 15:23).

OPEN WINDOWS AND DOORS

In my story in chapter 1, after Joe killed the egg-stealing snake and delivered the egg back to the hen, he set out to find the hole in the hen house. Leaving an opening meant more predators would get in and steal more eggs or kill chicks.

God placed Adam in the Garden of Eden with dominion over it to keep it prospering and protected. When Adam discovered that the "old serpent" had been whispering to his wife, he had the authority to kick it out—but he chose not to do so.

Instead, Adam chose to rebel against the specific instruction God gave him not to eat of the tree of the knowledge of good and evil (Gen. 2:17). Sin found a way into that garden and enticed Eve through her mind, will, and emotions.

Genesis 3:6 tells us that Eve "saw that the tree was good for food, that it was pleasant to the eyes, and a tree desirable to make one wise." Satan went after the soul, to sway her decision. He tempted her with something better. Notice this temptation is rooted in pride, the very thing that brought him down.

Many people who claim to be Christians try to conform the Word of God to fit their lives rather than conforming their lives to the Word of God.

Eve was deceived, but not Adam. He could have put an end to it, but he joined in instead.

Take a look at your life right now. Is there a hole in the fence, a broken window, or maybe a wide-open front door?

A father is the spiritual leader of the home. My father went to be with the Lord on September 17, 1991. I miss him deeply, but I was so blessed to have a dad like him. He loved God and he loved his family, and that dictated his thoughts and actions. He led our family by example, and the way he lived his life greatly impacted mine. I still feel the shadow of his influence on my life today.

I realize that not every man or woman has had a godly upbringing. Some of you have had horrendous experiences from absent or abusive parents. Even if that is the case, the Lord can completely redeem the time, heal the pain, and equip you to lead your family. And it's vital that you let Him do so.

When a father doesn't take his role seriously, it is one of those decisions that empower the enemy. He is quite happy to walk in the dominion that we forfeit. When you participate in those little dirty jokes on the job, you are empowering the wrong kingdom. When you listen to musical pornography, you are empowering the wrong kingdom. When you look at sexually explicit filth in movies, magazines, or on Internet sites, you are empowering the wrong kingdom. Maybe you don't actively participate in any of these things, but neither do you actively step up and lead your family in godly love and authority. You are empowering the wrong kingdom.

The same is true for mothers. When either parent gets mad or throws a temper tantrum, you are giving place to the devil. When you choose to harbor anger and resentment, you are empowering the wrong kingdom. That is why Paul warned, "Be angry, and do not sin: do not let the sun go down on your wrath" (Eph. 4:26).

That reminds me of a story about a man and a woman who had been married for sixty years. They were asked about their secret to staying together and happy for so long. The wife answered, "We made an agreement when we first got married that we absolutely would obey the Word of God and never let the sun go down on our wrath. If we got mad, we just wouldn't go to sleep until we got it right. It worked!"

Then the husband chimed in, "Yeah! It worked, but there were a lot of nights when we sat up all night and got mighty tired getting it right."

It's a humorous little story, but it illustrates a powerful,

powerful truth. The decisions we make each day as husbands and wives, as fathers and mothers, will affect the spiritual atmosphere of our homes.

If you looked out your window and saw hundreds of deadly snakes crawling around your house, you would make every effort to be sure there were no nooks and crannies for any of those snakes to get in. It is even more important to do this in the spirit realm.

The wisest man in the world, Solomon, said, "Like a city whose walls are broken down is a man who lacks self-control" (Prov. 25:28, NIV). Ancient cities typically had a protective wall around the perimeter for protection from thieves and evildoers.

When you have no self-control, you leave yourself and your home open for anything to attack. The devil doesn't even need a foothold in a situation like that. Demons can come and go freely through the doors you've left open to them.

The Power of the Tongue

Several of the things Paul mentions in Ephesians 4 that are connected to the old self—falsehood, lying, anger, bitterness, unwholesome talk, rage, brawling, slander—have to do with what we speak. Do not make the mistake of thinking that your words are not as serious as your actions. Proverbs 18:21 clearly states, "Death and life are in the power of the tongue."

Remember, we do not fight with the *carnal* weapons of the enemy (2 Cor. 10:4). When you use "carnal weapons," you are empowering the devil. When you get angry at someone, when you feel provoked to argue, do you have self-control—or do you just let it all go? Love is not easily provoked (1 Cor. 13:5).

The enemy watches for you to lose self-control because that is a soul decision that empowers him. Have you ever found yourself in situations where you felt like you just couldn't take anymore? Situations like that seem to justify letting someone have it, but that means you are letting unrenewed thoughts, insecurities, and unrestrained emotions lead you instead of the Spirit of God. The next thing you know, your tongue is giving power to the wrong kingdom. An atmosphere in the home where there is constant bickering, fussing, and feuding empowers the wrong kingdom. It opens the door to the python and invites him to start squeezing the life out of everyone who lives there.

It spills over into the church family as well. An atmosphere of disunity is very attractive to the enemy. People in churches can get into squabbles over things that don't amount to a hill of frostbitten Kentucky beans. But because of pride, the simplest disputes can escalate into very ugly arguments and division.

Just as unity brings God's presence, disunity in a home and in a church will dispel it. The devil loves getting a family or a church divided because division leads to destruction. And one of the fastest ways to create disunity is linked directly to the tongue: talking about others behind their backs. It's been said that a plastic surgeon can do almost anything with the human nose except keep it out of other people's business. Gossip might not start with you—but it should certainly *stop* with you.

> An atmosphere in the home where there is constant bickering, fussing, and feuding empowers the wrong kingdom.

Self-control applies to the tongue as well as to the emotions. "Keep your heart with all diligence, for out of it spring the issues of life" (Prov. 4:23). You can speak life into your family and into your church, or you can speak death. Guard your heart and guard your mouth. The next time you're tempted to say something unwholesome, to gossip, argue, or criticize—even if it seems justified—remember that it is better to turn the issue over to God than to empower the wrong kingdom and let the snakes in.

WHOM DO YOU EMPOWER?

God never intended for His church to walk in *less* power than it did in the beginning. The more we press into His presence, the *more* power we should see released in our lives! We were never designed to walk around defeated and oppressed, squeezed by the python in a demonically charged atmosphere.

Jesus promised, "For where two or three are gathered together in My name, I am there in the midst of them" (Matt. 18:20). Where populations ignore the Lord and choose to live lascivious, sinful lifestyles, their choices invite and empower the presence of demons.

As I said in chapter 3, a sustained atmosphere creates a climate, then a climate creates a stronghold. The stronghold defines the culture of a place. There are concentrations of demonic atmospheres across America where cities have become drug strongholds, sex-trafficking strongholds, homosexual strongholds, crime strongholds, abortion strongholds, and so on.

The continual work of sin in our nation is empowering the devil, and we are becoming the greatest pagan nation in the world as a result. It's time to recognize the enemy's agenda to squeeze the life out of us.

Just as the devil's kingdom is empowered by idolatry and ungodliness—the power of God's kingdom is manifested when we pray, worship, and live holy lives. We need to take the power back!

Just west of the shores of Scotland lies a string of small islands known as the Hebrides. A mighty revival spread across those islands from 1949 to 1952. Why those tiny little islands? What was significant about them? Two old ladies and some young deacons were humble enough to cry out to God and change the atmosphere.

Christine and Peggy Smith were in their eighties and too crippled to attend church regularly. They didn't let that stop them, however. Those two ladies maintained such an atmosphere of worship and prayer in their home that they met with God right there. The two became burdened for the souls of the young people of the islands because they were becoming indifferent to the gospel.

In prayer one night they sensed the Lord give them a promise from Isaiah 44:3, "For I will pour water on him who is thirsty, and floods on the dry ground; I will pour My Spirit on your descendants, and My blessing on your offspring." The sisters began to pray that promise and had a vision of the church filled with young people. They shared it with the elders, and several began to meet in a nearby barn to wait on the Lord.

One night the deacons became convicted after reading from Psalm 24:3–4: "Who may ascend into the hill of the Lord? Or who may stand in His holy place? He who has clean hands and a pure heart, who has not lifted up his soul to an idol, nor sworn deceitfully." They repented, and the Holy Spirit swept through that barn in a fresh and powerful way.

Duncan Campbell went to preach there for ten days, but he stayed for more than two years. Roughly 75 percent of the inhabitants of those islands were saved in those three years.[1] Talk about changing the atmosphere!

We need to recognize the One in us who is greater than the enemy. It is time to humble ourselves before Him, repent of self-will, stubbornness, and everything in our lives that offers the devil a safe harbor or foothold. That is the only way to break the python's chokehold in our homes, our churches, and our cities.

No Open Doors

Jesus said, "I will no longer talk much with you, for the ruler of this world is coming, and he has nothing in Me" (John 14:30). Jesus was sinless. There was nothing in Him for the accuser of the brethren to accuse or condemn. There was no foothold. There was no open door to the enemy through anger, bitterness, or strife.

After His arrest, Jesus told Pilate, "My kingdom is not of this world. If My kingdom were of this world, My servants would fight, so that I should not be delivered to the Jews; but now My kingdom is not from here" (John 18:36). Jesus was not conformed to this world but to the kingdom of God. There was no place for the python to wrap himself around Jesus and try to choke the life out of Him.

That is why Paul tells us not to be conformed to this world but be transformed by the renewing of our minds (Rom. 12:2). We have to put off the old self and *renew our minds* so that we give no foothold to the devil, so that we leave no open doors for the python and his brood of vipers to enter into our lives.

The power of God is released when believers choose not to be conformed to the world's ways but be transformed in their minds, wills, and emotions by God's Word. Paul said in

Romans 1:16 that he wasn't ashamed of the gospel of Christ because it is the power of God to salvation for everyone who believes.

Do you know when a church is its most powerful? When people become unashamed. When a church preaches the gospel of Jesus Christ and souls are regularly saved—that is a powerful church!

I travel and preach all over the world. Every time I am in a church that is a soul-winning church, there is power. The presence of God is there because His kingdom is being made manifest on the earth. The chains of sin and death are being broken. The grip of the python is being broken.

When you become unashamed, you empower the kingdom of light. I am not ashamed of the power of God and the gifts of the Spirit because it is what this world needs. There is power in the name of Jesus, and He has given us dominion in this world.

Stop giving Satan entrance into your life, your family, and your church. Stop giving him all the power by letting him gain footholds in your home. When you let in little sins here and there that seem harmless, just like a python those sins wrap themselves around you and slowly squeeze the breath out of you—and they all start as little eggs.

five

GET THE SNAKE EGGS OUT!

PYTHONS CAN LAY more eggs than any other breed of snake. One Burmese python is reported to have laid 107 eggs at one time![1] In most cases, after they lay their eggs, females will typically incubate them until they hatch. Since consistent temperature is critical for the snake embryos to develop, the female python incubates her eggs by coiling around them and shivering. This raises her body temperature and warms the eggs.[2]

What does this mini biology lesson on python eggs have to do with our Christian walk? Every sin begins with a thought. When James taught about temptation, he said each of us is tempted when we are drawn away by our own desires. "Then, when desire has conceived, it gives birth to sin; and sin, when it is full-grown, brings forth death" (James 1:15).

Although I've spent a great deal of time in this book explaining spiritual warfare, I want to say something that might sound surprising: the greatest battle for your soul is *not* the war going on between angels and demons; it is the war going on in between your ears. The battle starts with how you think and the "snake eggs" you allow the enemy to lay in your head.

Brutal mass killings in America are tragically becoming more common as of late. These horrific events have stirred major controversies over gun violence and gun laws. I'm not here to enter that debate, but I will tell you that taking all the guns away will not take care of the problem because the "snake eggs" will still exist.

The young men who shot up their high school years ago did not suddenly come up with the idea. Neither did the man who shot innocent victims at a movie theater. Like the man who slaughtered innocent children and adults in Connecticut, they had been carrying around those demonically inspired thoughts for weeks, maybe months, perhaps even years—like eggs waiting to hatch.

> The greatest battle for your soul is not the war going on between angels and demons; it is the war going on in between your ears.

It starts with a thought, and that thought is like an egg that Satan puts in your head. I often call these snake eggs "thought bombs." The problem is, eggs hatch.

A Snake's Nest in Your Head

How does the python lay his snake eggs in your life? He gains access through your eyes, your ears, and your mouth. The things you allow yourself to watch, to hear, and to speak profoundly affect the spiritual atmosphere of your life. Before Satan can overcome you, he must get a temptation in your mind.

Remember the devil trying to tempt Jesus after His forty-day fast in the wilderness? The devil had already struck out twice. After the third attempt Jesus said, "Away with you, Satan!" (Matt. 4:10). Luke wrote that the devil "departed from Him until an opportune time" (Luke 4:13).

Life is not about going along with the crowd, but rather taking a stand for righteousness. It is a dangerous thing to toy with temptation and let your mind wander. It seems harmless enough to wonder what it would be like to have a relationship with your married coworker. After all, if it is just a thought, then you're not hurting anyone, right? Wrong. As you look at that coworker and think those thoughts, you allow the python to lay those eggs in your mind.

That's why Jesus said, "Whoever looks at a woman to lust for her has already committed adultery with her in his heart" (Matt. 5:28). What you look at and dwell on incubates those python eggs. Job was so passionate about honoring the Lord in all things that he said, "I made a covenant with my eyes not to look lustfully at a girl" (Job 31:1, NIV).

Too bad Abraham's nephew Lot didn't make the same type of covenant. Lot wanted to take his flocks and his riches and move out on his own. So Lot and his family set out toward the city of Sodom and pitched their tents facing the city of sin. Every morning when he woke up, that city was the first thing Lot saw. Every night when he went to bed, it was the last thing he saw.

Before long he was sitting in the gate of the city (Gen. 19:1). Instead of a tent on the outskirts of town, he had moved closer. The thing he was looking at was drawing him closer to a life-style of sin.

Your life will always move in the direction of the dominant images you allow to reside in your mind. Those images become thoughts that will eventually become actions.

You've probably heard the old saying, "You can't stop a bird from flying over your head, but you don't have to let it nest in your hair." You can't always control what appears before your eyes, but you can control how long you look. You can't control every thought that comes into your mind, but you can control how long you dwell on that thought.

The culture of our country is moving us farther and farther away from God. Even those who are trying to stand against the flow of wickedness are subtly affected by sounds and images. The prevalence of the Internet only increases the bombardment of our eyes, ears, and thoughts with lewdness and iniquity.

> Your life will always move in the direction of the dominant images you allow to reside in your mind.

What are you watching? To what and to whom are you listening? Images and thoughts will try to get in—but you don't have to let them stay. "Let the wicked forsake his way, and the unrighteous man his thoughts; let him return to the LORD, and He will have mercy on him; and to our God, for He will abundantly pardon" (Isa. 55:7).

Remember, if a python stops incubating the eggs in its nest, they will die. Kick the python out. Don't let that snake make a nest and hatch his eggs in your mind.

GOD SEES WHAT YOU DO IN DARKNESS

In my years of preaching there have been several times when I felt the weight of something the Lord wanted me to share, almost in a tangible way. What the Holy Spirit showed me about the following verses was one of those times. God was leading the prophet Ezekiel through a vision to see the wickedness of the people.

He said to me, "Son of man, do you see what they are doing, the great abominations that the house of Israel commits here, to make Me go far away from My sanctuary? Now turn again, you will see greater abominations."

So He brought me to the door of the court; and when I looked, there was a hole in the wall. Then He said to me, "Son of man, dig into the wall"; and when I dug into the wall, there was a door. And He said to me, "Go in, and see the wicked abominations which they are doing there." So I went in and saw, and there— every sort of creeping thing, abominable beasts, and all the idols of the house of Israel, portrayed all around on the walls. And there stood before them seventy men of the elders of the house of Israel, and in their midst stood Jaazaniah the son of Shaphan. Each man had a censer in his hand, and a thick cloud of incense went up. Then He said to me, "Son of man, have you seen what the elders of the house of Israel do in the dark, every man in the room of his idols? For they say, 'The LORD does not see us, the LORD has forsaken the land.'"

—EZEKIEL 8:6–12

Seventy elders served in the house of Israel. They were descendants of the same seventy elders who were chosen to serve with Moses seventeen generations earlier. But by this time all had fallen away from serving the purposes of God and began serving perversion instead. They went from being pure and holy before God and serving in His temple to looking at pornography on the walls and offering incense before the images.

Some Bible historians point to this vision as the first mention of pornography in the Bible. The interior walls of the temple were painted with lewd, wicked, perverted images of beasts and idols. God said, "They think I don't see and I don't know what they do in darkness, in their 'hidden' chambers."

God sees what you do in darkness. You cannot look at pornography in the secrecy of your home office, in the dark of night, and expect the presence of God to be near you. The atmosphere you live in either attracts the presence of God or drives Him away.

We live in a pornographic world, and America is smitten with smut. Our generation is submerged in a hellish tide of impurity. I was astonished when I read the following pornography statistics:[3]

- Every second $3,075.64 is being spent on pornography.

- Every second 28,258 Internet users are viewing pornography.

- In that same second 372 Internet users are typing adult search terms into search engines.

- Every thirty-nine minutes a new pornographic video is being created in the United States.

Understand that you and I are visual beings. That means your eyes can take in 4 million bytes of information per second at the speed of 187,000 miles per second. Your mind automatically converts words into pictures. If I say I am about to bite into a big red apple, you can envision one in your mind. The same thing happens if I say black dog or white horse.

Jesus said, "The lamp of the body is the eye. If therefore your eye is good, your whole body will be full of light. But if your eye is bad, your whole body will be full of darkness. If therefore the light that is in you is darkness, how great is that darkness!" (Matt. 6:22–23).

The eyes and ears of millions are being polluted. Your eye lets light into your whole body, but if your eye is corrupt, your whole body will be corrupt. You may think you are hiding it in your "secret chamber," but the effects are not hidden. The enemy is filling the atmosphere of your home each time you click.

Christians must wake up! Many are filling their eyes and minds with sexual images in the comfort of their own homes. They are thinking about it, playing it over and over in their minds, and eventually acting on it. Watching pornography and sexually explicit TV shows and movies is like getting a blood transfusion straight from hell. Thought bombs are constantly being thrown at us.

It's not difficult to see how Satan is using the world of entertainment to advance his kingdom. Movies are blatantly mocking our Christian faith. Television shows are filled with unmarried couples in and out of bedrooms. Profanity, sex, and at least partial nudity are common. From cartoons to comedy, the mindbenders use television shows, movies, and music to channel us into the mold of the world's thinking.

Be careful if you think that just because your kids are in youth group every Sunday and Wednesday night none of this applies to them. I believe the devil targets church kids more than any other kids. Once those thought bombs get into the mind, if they are given safe harbor there, it is only a matter of time before they are hatched and acted out.

It is the same with some of the music that is produced today. Satan is the great mind manipulator, and he works subliminally through music. Your kids are being bombarded and don't even know what's hitting them. I'm not trying to blast all modern music, but I think we should be aware of the fact that Satan can use it as his tool to pull us away from God and into chaotic thinking. The ability of music to excite and ignite wrong thinking is very real. More often than not these days, the lyrics of the biggest hits are so lewd they may as well be labeled as porn. The words lead to mental images, and another egg is hatched.

> Watching pornography and sexually explicit TV shows and movies is like getting a blood transfusion straight from hell.

The same thing happens when a young person starts wondering what it would be like to start smoking, drinking, or doing hard drugs. They see it, they spend time thinking about it, and the first time the opportunity is available, they are hooked.

Parents, be vigilant! Don't leave openings in your home for the python to come in and lay eggs in the minds of your kids. Talk to them. Make sure they understand the price of empowering the wrong kingdom. Take smoking, for instance. If every cigarette smoked takes three minutes off your life, then the average smoker loses about fifteen years. Marijuana has been shown to have even more potent life-shortening effects since it releases five times the carbon monoxide into the bloodstream and twice the level of carcinogens into the lungs. That makes smoking a joint equivalent to smoking a whole pack of (twenty) cigarettes.[4]

What makes addiction to these things so inconceivable is that God gave man dominion over *all* the animals and plants of the earth (Gen. 1:26–30). What does tobacco come from?

What about cocaine and marijuana? They come from plants. Even alcohol is distilled or fermented from plants. Things are totally backward when you have people walking around stoned and inebriated—under the dominion of plants—when we were created to have dominion instead.

THE SNAKE EGG OF DOUBT

Some may think it fashionable to doubt. In your circle of friends, for instance, doubt may seem to be a badge of intellectual superiority. The devil uses the snake egg of doubt on everyone he can. He even used this subtle device in the temptation of Jesus Christ in Luke 4. When you read that scripture, you'll notice that the devil said, *"If* you are the Son of God..." If? If? If?

It's worth noting that the first question mark in the Bible did not come from God; it came from Satan. In the Garden of Eden the serpent said to Eve, "Has God said...?" If Satan can get you to begin to question—"Did God really say that?" "Does God love me?" "Does God really answer prayer?" "Is God's Word really true?"—then he can win in your life.

The old serpent's first words in the Old Testament were, "Has God said?" But by contrast, the first words of Jesus recorded in the New Testament are, "It is written." Jesus took Satan's question of "Has God said?" and turned it into a declaration of "God *has* said!"

Picture the shape of a question mark in your mind. A question mark is just an exclamation point that has been bent out of shape. Change your question mark to an exclamation point, and say to every snake egg of doubt, "It is written!"

This is not a time to doubt your beliefs and believe your doubts. It's time to feed your faith and starve your fears. Don't allow Satan to clip your wings of faith with his scissors of reason. Don't let the python persuade you that it just doesn't do any good to pray or that reading your Bible is no longer important. Believe the Bible, and hold on to your faith.

Doubt needs to be recognized for what it is: a spiritual battle. A spiritual battle must be fought with spiritual weapons. Just as he tried to make Eve doubt what God had said in the Garden of Eden, Satan wants you to doubt God's Word. Doubt is still one of the most effective devices he uses.

Evolution is one of those snake eggs that the python lays to work doubt into the minds of people. Darwin introduced what seemed to be a scientific basis for not believing in a creation God. The impact of this thought bomb is that since man had no special beginning, he has no purpose or destiny. This thinking leads many to sink into wasted, unproductive lives, and it leads others into rejecting the existence of the God of the universe.

> This is not a time to doubt your beliefs and believe your doubts. It's time to feed your faith and starve your fears.

Believing that humans are the result of evolution is just as ridiculous as believing a Rolex watch is a happy accident. Let's say you find a Rolex on the sidewalk, but instead of believing it has been created for a purpose, you believe that the mines of Africa mined themselves and somehow a gold casing perfectly designed for this watch crossed the ocean and found itself lying there on the sidewalk. Then springs just bounced on over from the Massachusetts Institute of Technology and fell in place inside the watch by accident. Then the remaining interior parts of the watch appeared and began working properly and precisely to keep perfect time—again, just by sheer luck. Next the glass facing for the watch blew around in the wind all the way from Pittsburgh until it fell into place. Lastly, I wonder how you would explain the diamonds. Maybe they were dropped accidentally by a jewel thief after his heist and they landed perfectly on the face of the watch on the sidewalk.

Do you believe any of that could happen? I don't. And if we don't believe something like a watch came into existence by chance, how can we possibly believe that human beings or other parts of creation happened by accident either? You and I are infinitely more complex in our makeup than a Rolex watch—not to mention that we are alive rather than being inanimate. I believe that we were created and given life by the only One who had the power to raise Himself from the grave.

Science may try and fill our minds with elaborate explanations of a protoplasm that wiggled around until it became fish; fish that grew legs and walked out on land where it grew fur and ate leaves, then it grew a tail to hang from the tree limbs. Eventually the tail and the fur fell off, and the monkey evolved into a human.

Now, my great-great-great-great-granddaddy may have hung from a tree by his neck, but he never hung from a tree by his tail! Some people seem to get educated beyond reasonable intelligence. I heard a story about one student who, after his professor taught on evolution, asked if he could share a poem that he had written on the subject. The professor proudly gave permission. The young man stood and read:

> In the beginning, it was microbe beginning to begin.
> And then it was a tadpole with its tail tucked in.
> And then it was a monkey climbing up in a tree.
> But now it's a professor with a PhD.

I don't know if the professor was particularly amused, but I do know that it takes more faith to believe evolution than it does to believe "In the beginning God created the heavens and the earth." I choose to believe the living Word of God over the philosophies and theories of man.

Remember those doctrines of demons that I mentioned in chapter 3? People find themselves lured into false religions when they open the doors to the python and he lays eggs of doubt in their minds. A trusted leader twists the Word of God to make it fit the culture. Friends say you are being too closed-minded and need to understand and experiment with other religions. Popular celebrities make fashionable religions out of Scientology, Buddhism, Islam, New Age, Kabbalah, and the list goes on and on.

Paul was very concerned over the Gentile churches being lured into false religions and cults that were so pervasive in the society in his day. He wrote to the Colossians, "See to it that no one takes you captive through hollow and deceptive philosophy, which depends on human tradition and the basic principles of this world rather than on Christ" (Col. 2:8, NIV). Always guard your heart *and* keep your mind renewed through the reading of God's Word.

CRACK SOME EGGS!

On August 18, 1969, five people were murdered at the home of a wealthy movie producer. The marks on Sharon Tate and Jay Sebring indicated that the murders bore some sort of ritualistic significance, a fact later confirmed by witnesses who were members of the notorious Manson Family. This group of young people lived on the edge of Death Valley in the desert of California. They had sworn allegiance to Charles Manson, a deranged man who had introduced them to drugs and sex orgies and commanded killings of shocking brutality.

Charles Manson and the Manson Family slaughtered pregnant Sharon Tate along with four other victims. Sharon Tate was a movie star and her husband, Roman Polanski, was one of the first Hollywood producers to explore the occult in film. His hit movie *Rosemary's Baby* was about a satanic cult and brought satanic rituals to the big screen for one of the first times in the United States. Back in the early seventies this was shocking, and it opened the doors to other films such as *The Exorcist*.

If you read quotes from a 1969 interview, it's easy to see that Polanski's goal was to expose the open minds of the next generation to the occult.[5] After watching the movie, the Manson family invaded his home and tortured and slaughtered his wife and guests. I wonder if it occurred to this movie producer that everything begins with a thought. One of the descriptions of a wicked person is given in Romans 1, where Paul says they became "futile in their thoughts, and their foolish hearts were darkened" (v. 21).

Another scripture says, "Every intent of the thoughts of his [man's] heart was only evil continually" (Gen. 6:5). The Manson family had all watched *Rosemary's Baby*, and ironically the thoughts it planted in their minds led to the deaths of Polanski's wife and friends and several other innocent victims.

Watch your thought life. It all begins with a thought! But God is looking for people who will invite Him into the "secret chambers" to clean out all the thought bombs and filth.

It is time to crack some eggs! It is time to fight with the knowledge that "the weapons of our warfare are not carnal but mighty in God for pulling down strongholds, casting down arguments and every high thing that exalts itself against the knowledge of God, bringing every thought into captivity to the obedience of Christ" (2 Cor. 10:4–5). It is time to clean out the snake nests we've allowed in the secret places of our hearts and minds and create a habitation for God.

I once heard a story about a Native American on a reservation who gave his heart to the Lord and was born again. He went to his pastor a few weeks later and said "Pastor, I have a problem. Now that I'm saved, every day I feel there is an internal fight going on in my mind. It's like there is a white dog and a black dog fighting each other to the death."

The old wise pastor understood the new convert was referring to the invisible war that we all fight between our new nature that feeds on the Word of God and spiritual things and the old nature that feeds on the lust of the flesh, the lust of the eyes, and the pride of life. The wise old pastor asked the man, "So Joe, which dog wins the fight?"

The man paused for a moment and said, "You know, I never thought about it before, but the dog I feed the most wins the fight."

The same is true for you and me. When it comes to the battle for your thought life, if you feed your carnal nature on impure thoughts, then that dog will win the battle for your thought life. On the other hand, if you feed the new nature you have been given on the Word of God, uplifting messages, and wholesome thoughts, then your new nature will defeat the power of temptation to sin. (See Philippians 4:8.)

Which dog are you feeding the most? That's the one that will win the fight! Which snake eggs are you allowing to hatch? Those are the thought bombs that will take over your mind and begin to rule your actions.

If this chapter has spoken to your heart and you know there are things you've been allowing yourself to dwell on that need to be cleaned out, don't put it off by telling yourself that God doesn't know and doesn't see. He knows. He sees. He is ready to wash you and purge you of any unclean thoughts so you can set your mind on things above.

Wherever you are right now as you read this book, forget about everybody around you and pray, "God, here are the secret chambers of my life. I want You to be more than the Lord of my public life. I want you to be Lord of my private life. Clean me out. Fill me with the Holy Ghost and use me for Your glory."

If you prayed that prayer, I know that the Lord heard you, forgave you, and filled you with His Spirit to empower you to defeat the python in your life and home.

In this first section of the book you've learned about your enemy, the devil, and his demons who are engaged in a very real spiritual battle for your soul. You've also learned about some of the ways you may unknowingly allow this sly snake access into your life and mind.

In the next section I'll uncover more in-depth python strategies of the devil and the ways he tries to choke your breath, stifle your prayer life, mute your praise, limit your life, and silence your voice. Exposing his evil schemes is the next step to defeating him, so read on!

THE PYTHON'S PLAN TO SQUEEZE THE LIFE OUT OF YOU

six

CHOKING YOUR BREATH

I N THE NATURAL a python's mode of killing his prey is different from that of any other snake. The python doesn't poison his victim with venom; instead, he encircles his intended prey and tightens his grip until the last bit of air is expelled. A python is designed to stop breath.

As you realize by now, the purpose of this book is to show you the many ways that the devil and his demons employ the same strategy in our lives. Their number one priority is to squeeze the spiritual breath out of us.

There are four distinct times that the Bible says, "God breathed." The first is in Genesis 2:7, where we read that God reached into the dirt and formed the first man, Adam. The Hebrew word for "breath" in this verse is *neshamah,* which literally means "air inhaled and exhaled." This means God inhaled and exhaled in the garden and He created man.

Almighty God put His mouth on that lump of dirt and shared His breath with him, making Adam a living being in His own image. We're not here by chance; we're here because God breathed the breath of life into us. He created us as rational beings who could choose to love and to follow God, or to reject Him. Right away the serpent slithered in to twist the truth, spread deception, and choke the life out of man through sin.

The second time that the Bible mentions the breath of God is found in 2 Timothy 3:16–17, when Paul explained that, "All Scripture is given by inspiration of God, and is profitable for doctrine, for reproof, for correction, for instruction in righteousness, that the man of God may be complete, thoroughly equipped for every good work."

The word *inspiration* is translated from the Greek word *theópneustos*, (*theós*, which means "God," and *pnéo*, which means "breathe out"). The words of Scripture were divinely inspired, or "breathed out" by God through the Holy Spirit; "No prophecy of Scripture is of any private interpretation, for prophecy never came by the will of man, but holy men of God spoke as they were moved by the Holy Spirit" (2 Pet. 1:20–21). The Bible is literally God-breathed.

Men like Moses, the prophets, and the disciples experienced the breath of God—that divine anointing that allowed His heart to be recorded for eternity. Isaiah would be sitting around when suddenly the breath of God would come on him and he would begin to write under the anointing.

Approximately forty different men put together the Bible over a span of about fifteen hundred years. Isn't it amazing that the words of all of those different prophets and writers fit perfectly together over a fifteen-hundred-year span? Think about it for a minute: most of them would have had no way of knowing what the others were writing, and yet all of them say the same thing, and the shadows and types fit perfectly together because God breathed life into His Book. That is why the Bible is not like any other book.

The writer of the Book of Hebrews said, "The word of God is living and active. Sharper than any double-edged sword, it penetrates even to dividing soul and spirit, joints and marrow;

it judges the thoughts and attitudes of the heart" (Heb. 4:12, NIV).

So in the Old Testament we find God breathing to create man and breathing again to give us His Word, the Bible. But there comes a third time when the breath of God shows up on the planet. In the New Testament Jesus opened the way for the Holy Spirit to be *in* the men and women of God.

After His resurrection Jesus appeared to Mary Magdalene in the garden, and then to the disciples. Jesus spoke with them and commissioned them to be His witnesses, speaking forth His words with anointing and power. As He did, "He breathed on them, and said to them, 'Receive the Holy Spirit'" (John 20:22).

Just as God breathed life into Adam in the garden, Jesus breathed on His disciples. He sent them out with the power and anointing of His words in their mouths. That power of the Holy Spirit is what enables us to live spiritually. It is what enables us to not only *hear* the Word but to *do* the Word.

You can't keep this Word just by thinking and trying in the natural; it takes the breath of God filling you with His life. And when His life is inside of you, then you can live the Word. When His life is inside of you, then you can keep His commandments.

Many people try to change themselves so that they can deserve God's grace and God's goodness. Only when you are born again and receive that breath of life from the Lord through the Holy Spirit does that change take place.

There is one other time that the life-giving breath of God is mentioned in Scripture. It's in the Old Testament Book of Ezekiel, but I believe it gives us a picture of another way the breath of God comes forth in our lives today.

In chapter 37 the prophet Ezekiel found himself in a large valley. When he looked around, the ground as far as he could see was covered with piles of human bones that were disjointed and dried in the sun. God asked Ezekiel if the bones could live. He wisely answered, "O LORD God, You know" (v. 3). In other words, Ezekiel had no clue how it could happen.

The situation must have looked utterly hopeless to the natural eye. But Ezekiel knew God had a plan. So the Lord told him to prophesy to the bones.

There are several interpretations of what this passage means pertaining to Israel and the church in the end times, but I also see another meaning. I believe this passage simply and beautifully illustrates the breath of God bringing life into dead, hopeless situations. Instead of a valley littered with disjointed, sun-bleached bones, it became alive with an army full of the breath of God that brings life out of death and hope out of hopelessness.

There are times when the python wraps hopelessness around your life to the point that you feel like you can't take another breath. Understand that hopelessness is a deception of the enemy! He is wrapping you up in his crushing coils. He intends to destroy—but God intends to make you alive.

IT'S ALL ABOUT RELATIONSHIP

The same breath of God that brought Adam to life also brought Ezekiel's dry bones to life, breathed the Holy Spirit onto the disciples, and inspired every word of the Bible. God's Word brings life to your spirit when you begin to partake of it; it's like breathing in the breath of God. In other words, reading your Bible is like breathing His breath into your spirit. Remember in chapter 2 when I explained that your spiritual breath is made up of reading the Word of God (inhaling) and prayer (exhaling)? Without physical breathing your body would die; without spiritual breath your spirit man dies. It's what connects you to an intimate relationship with the Lord.

It's a sad but true fact that many people in our churches do not have an intimate relationship with Jesus Christ. They may experience His presence during a powerful worship service, but during the week they are barren, cold, and empty on the inside. They've stopped breathing, spiritually speaking. They haven't entered into an intimate relationship with God.

Jesus had His own relationship with the Father. Many times in the Gospels we read about Him separating Himself in order to spend time alone in prayer. Even Jesus needed to stay connected to the source of life. He said, "Most assuredly, I say to you, the Son can do nothing of Himself, but what He sees the Father do; for whatever He does, the Son also does in like manner. For the Father loves the Son, and shows Him all things that He Himself does; and He will show Him greater works than these, that you may marvel" (John 5:19–20).

Somehow we have developed a concept of Jesus being "so much God" that He never had a human problem, never faced a human dilemma, never came under the attack of the enemy, or felt what you and I feel. He was not just "wholly God"; He was also "wholly man."

Speaking about Jesus, the Bible says that He can sympathize with our weaknesses, because He was tempted in all the same ways we are, yet He didn't fall into sin (Heb. 4:15). He was aware of the emotional roller coaster some experience. He was aware of the temptations of the enemy to live according to the flesh rather than according to the Spirit. He knew what we would experience, and *yet* He did not let those things rule over

Him. He had to maintain His relationship with the Father just as you and I do.

Because Jesus was a human being, He is living proof that we have the opportunity to develop the same level of closeness to God. If Jesus was not a human being with the same passions and the same areas of need like me, then He could not be my pattern and my example. Jesus's relationship with the Father was so close and so revealing that Jesus could say, "The Father loves the Son and shows Him all things that He Himself does."

You do not reveal yourself to just anybody. You do not share the intimacies of your heart, the *real* you, with someone who is not that close. An intimate relationship is one that is close enough to feel the breath of the other. This is what the python-like tactics of the enemy work to cut off.

INTIMACY IS JUST THE BEGINNING

Intimacy with God is one of three distinct characteristics that marked the earthly relationship Jesus maintained with His Father: intimacy, dependency, and obedience. These three characteristics can also be found in the lives of men such as Moses, David, John, and Paul—and they should be in the life of every believer. Allow me to explain.

Intimacy

After spending forty days and nights in the presence of God, Moses was ready to go back down the mountain with God's laws, the Ten Commandments, for His people. When Moses came down from Mount Sinai with the two tablets of the Testimony in his hands, he was not aware that his face was radiant because he had spoken with the Lord. When Aaron and all the Israelites saw Moses, his face was radiant, and they were afraid to come near him. (See Exodus 34:29–30.) Moses didn't have to offer his credentials as proof of his calling. When he walked down off of that mountain, they could see how close he had been to God because even his countenance was changed.

Intimacy with the Lord requires alone time with just Him. I have a level of relationship with God in public, behind the pulpit, with my family, and friends. But intimacy comes in times of seeking His presence one on one.

If you want to know God's will for your life, He invites you to spend time with Him. He doesn't reveal Himself to strangers who stand afar off, but to His children.

An intimate relationship is one that is close enough to feel the breath of the other.

During Jesus's earthly ministry there were multitudes of people who followed Him for the miracles He performed. Then one day He invited them to be even closer. He told the crowd, "I am the bread of life. Your forefathers ate the manna in the desert, yet they died. But here is the bread that comes down from heaven, which a man may eat and not die. I am the living bread that came down from heaven. If anyone eats of this bread, he will live forever. This bread is my flesh, which I will give for the life of the world" (John 6:48–51, NIV). That was more than some could handle, and Scripture tells us that at that point many of His disciples turned away and no longer followed Him.

Twelve disciples stayed close to the Lord, and He chose to pour His life and teaching into them. Out of those twelve there were three who became even closer. And out of the three there was one, "John the beloved," who laid his head on Jesus's chest at their last meal together—close enough to hear the Lord's heart beating.

Three Keys to Intimacy with God

Three key things help you to develop intimacy: desire, discipline, and delight.

Desire: The Lord will begin to reveal Himself as you fellowship with Him. As I said earlier in this book, establish a place of meeting and wait for Him there. It is in the secret place that He reveals His will and plans for your life. He will not shout it across the room or break into your daily distractions to get your attention. You must desire intimacy with Him above everything else.

Discipline: You must desire intimacy with the Lord, and you must discipline yourself to have that time. You could say that it comes back to *atmosphere*. Do you spend time creating an atmosphere where the Lord is welcome or one where the enemy is welcome? If you want intimacy, you must discipline and renew your mind by the Word of God, by prayer, and by worshipping the Lord. God desires fellowship with you. He is waiting. But you must make the move to get alone with Him. All the distractions of life act like that python, slowly wrapping around and choking the breath out of your spiritual life.

Delight: You are less likely to discipline yourself to do something if you don't find any pleasure in the activity. What gets your attention the most? In what do you find the most pleasure? You may have phenomenal times of worship at your church or at special conferences or events you attend. However, your greatest times of worship should take place when you are alone with the Lord. Make it your goal to delight in His presence privately even more than you do publicly.

Dependency

After intimacy, the second characteristic of Jesus was dependency. Remember, Jesus said He could do "nothing of Himself" (John 5:19). Jesus was empowered by the Holy Spirit, but He chose to do what He saw the Father doing. He was dependent upon God for everything that He did.

We sing songs with phrases such as, "Without Him I can do nothing," yet we go out and try to do everything on our own. We work hard to become independent rather than dependent. That means we can only accomplish things with our own power rather than with God's power.

To the extent that you depend on yourself and what you can do, that's how much you defuse God's power in your life. If you're 50 percent depending on yourself, whether it's on your job or anything else, if you're 50 percent depending on your intellect and your ability to make it happen, that's 50 percent of God's power you won't have. The more dependent you are upon Him, the more He moves in and through your life.

Psalm 37:4 commands us to delight in the Lord. Verse 5 tells us to commit our way to the Lord and trust Him, and He will bring it to pass. It doesn't say, "Trust in your own ability to make it happen." When you are not dependent upon God, you will look *around* for the answer instead of looking *up*. David didn't tell us to trust in ourselves, in the financial planner, in the economy, or in the government. He didn't even tell us to trust in pastors or prophets. He didn't tell us to trust anything or anyone other than the Lord.

I am convinced that there are a lot of people God cannot use simply because they live as though they "have it all together" without Him. I like the way Paul put it,

Not many wise according to the flesh, not many mighty, not many noble, are called. But God has chosen the foolish things of the world to put to shame the wise, and God has chosen the weak things of the world to put to shame the things which are mighty; and the base things of the world and the things which are despised God has chosen, and the things which are not, to bring to nothing the things that are, that no flesh should glory in His presence.

—1 CORINTHIANS 1:26–29

I don't know about you, but that describes me pretty well. I don't often feel very wise, mighty, or noble. In fact, there are times when I feel like I fail God miserably. In the eyes of the world that spells failure. But in the eyes of God, it is exactly what He is looking for—those who will be dependent upon Him to do great and mighty things.

> To the extent that you depend on yourself and what you can do, that's how much you defuse God's power in your life.

One of the greatest things God has worked in my life is a dependency upon Him. I used to think that I could handle anything, but I've learned that I do not have the answers without Him.

You might want to check your dependency level. That python will slither in, whisper in your ear, separate you from God, and convince you that you have the charisma, the management skills, the people skills, and so forth to make it happen on your own. Without God there is no life in it.

Obedience

After Jesus spoke of intimacy and dependency, He talked of obedience: "I do not seek My own will but the will of the Father who sent Me" (John 5:30). Jesus never once consulted His own will. He never tried to please Himself. He lived to do the will of the Father.

Most of us do not understand that kind of obedience. What made the difference? Jesus believed that the Father was engineering all the circumstances of His life. That is a revelation that will change the way you live, and that revelation comes through intimacy.

The greater your intimacy with the Lord, the greater your trust. The greater your trust in the Lord, the greater your dependency. The greater your dependency on Him, the greater your obedience. He is in control of it all. If you understood that, you wouldn't grumble and complain so much. You would put an end to fussing and blaming God when things don't go as you think they should.

Jesus was sharing with His disciples, giving them "the keys of the kingdom of heaven" and telling them of His eminent death and resurrection. Peter, having just proclaimed that Jesus was the "Christ, the Son of the living God," of course, protested. After rebuking Peter, who momentarily lost focus on God's "bigger picture," Jesus said, "If anyone desires to come after Me, let him deny himself, and take up his cross, and follow Me" (Matt. 16:24).

Jesus could not live His life on His own—and He wanted His followers to understand that we cannot either. Jesus could not carry His own cross. After all He had endured, He came to a breaking point. That is what the cross does in each person's life. God will allow us to come to a breaking point on our own, but He will be there to help.

As I have come to this revelation personally, time and again, I have come to this conclusion: I am no longer on the throne. He is on the throne. He is engineering all the circumstances of my life. When I'm having a good day, it means that God is in control. When I have a bad day, a rough season, when my cross gets heavy, He is still in control and engineering my life.

The good news is, God wants us to succeed! Paul wrote the following words of encouragement to the Philippian church: "Therefore, my beloved, as you have always obeyed, not as in my presence only, but now much more in my absence, work out your own salvation with fear and trembling; for it is God who works in you both to will and to do for His good pleasure" (Phil. 2:12–13).

God is working obedience in your life. He is not just leaving it up to you to get around to it. He is going to keep working on you until your will comes in line with His will.

How do you work out your own salvation? The work of the cross purchased your salvation. Once God puts His will in you and begins to turn your will to want to do His pleasure, what He puts in, you have to work out.

Before Jesus was crucified, He prayed for His disciples and all who would follow Him in years to come. Then He said to God, "I have glorified You on the earth. I have finished the work which You have given Me to do" (John 17:4).

Jesus didn't begin His earthly ministry until He was thirty. Just three and a half years later He claimed to have finished everything God gave Him to do. How is that possible? He knew the confines of His area of ministry.

The enemy visited Jesus three times in the desert with three different temptations. Many scholars say those temptations were intended to be shortcuts to obeying the will of God. Jesus did not fall for it. Neither should you. Let God have His complete work and complete control of your life, and you will not fall prey to the squeeze of the python.

This progression of intimacy through God's Word, prayer, and praise that leads to trust and dependency on God followed by obedience is how you stay connected to the source of your spiritual life. It's your spiritual breath, and it's what the python wants so desperately to choke. In the next few chapters we'll look at how he wants to silence your voice of prayer, stop your praise, and put limitations on other areas of your life. It's time to breathe again!

seven

SILENCING YOUR VOICE

JESUS SAID, "HE who believes in Me, as the Scripture has said, out of his heart will flow rivers of living water" (John 7:38). Your voice releases prayer. It releases praise. With your voice you proclaim the plans and purposes of God.

I recently asked a Hispanic friend of mine if his children speak Spanish. "No," he replied. "I wish they did. But to be honest, my wife and I don't speak Spanish around the house. We are just so busy that even though it's the language we were raised with and we are bilingual, our children never hear us use it in the car or in our home, so they don't know any Spanish. It's not even a second language in our home."

His answer struck me as an illustration of our spiritual voices. Our children have to hear us declaring our faith, speaking our prayers and praise, and demonstrating our relationship with Jesus. If the words we use in our homes don't model a Christian lifestyle, our children will never become fluent themselves. It has to be done daily. There's an interesting story in the book of Nehemiah that explains what I'm talking about.

Nehemiah discovered his language dying in Jerusalem. The people had broken the covenant of God, and as a result, the city was nearly destroyed. Only a small remnant remained when Nehemiah arrived to start rebuilding. He heard Hebrew children playing in the streets and noticed that they weren't speaking Hebrew: "In those days I also saw Jews who had married women of Ashdod, Ammon, and Moab. And half of their children spoke the language of Ashdod, and could not speak the language of Judah, but spoke according to the language of one or the other people" (Neh. 13:23–24).

The men had married women who worshipped other gods and the language of the children revealed the people's idolatry. When you read on, you see that Nehemiah was enraged by this discovery because the loss of the language meant the people of God were losing their culture.

The same thing is happening in Christian homes today. The enemy, acting like a python, is choking out the Word of the Lord in our homes. There is a generation being raised that can't speak the spiritual language of our forefathers. Even those who are "bilingual" are speaking about the things of God merely as a *second* language.

Christianity has become their second language, and the culture of our time is their first language. It's happening because in many homes, it's what they are exposed to the most. It's dangerous to families when the children learn to speak half Bible and half Oprah; half Word of God and half secular humanism; half living for Jesus and half living for the world.

The twenty-first-century church is marrying the spirit of this age and raising a generation of children who do not know the language of God, the language of the Holy Spirit. They don't know the language of praise and prayer that pulls down strongholds. This generation has adopted the language of the culture.

Yet Deuteronomy 6:4–7 gives clear instruction about our language: "Hear, O Israel: The LORD our God, the LORD is one! You shall love the LORD your God with all your heart, with all your soul, and with all your strength. And these words which I command you today shall be in your heart. You shall teach them diligently to your children, and shall talk of them when you sit in your house, when you walk by the way, when you lie down, and when you rise up."

It's not enough to speak the language in church once a week. It has to be spoken fluently in the home if you expect your children to learn and speak it. The next generation will never speak what we don't speak.

Remember what Jesus said: "For I have not spoken on My own authority; but the Father who sent Me gave Me a command, what I should say and what I should speak" (John 12:49). Even Jesus spoke what He heard His Father speak.

Revelation 12:11 tells us, "And they overcame him by the blood of the Lamb and by the word of their testimony, and they did not love their lives to the death." Do not allow the python to choke the language of God out of your home. If you allow him to wrap his way around your life, he will silence your voice.

YOUR MOUTH IS YOUR GREATEST WEAPON!

A man named Thomas became a monk, joined a monastery, and took a vow of silence. The only exception to the vow was that once every ten years Thomas was called into the study of his superior, who said, "Brother Thomas, do you have anything to say?" At the end of Thomas's first decade of silence, his superior asked if he had anything to say. The monk replied, "The food is bad." Then he went back to his duties.

A decade passed. Again, Thomas was summoned to the study of his superior. "Brother Thomas," said the superior, "do you have anything to say?"

Thomas replied, "The bed is too hard." Then he went back to his duties.

Another decade passed. Again, Thomas was called in before his superior. "Brother Thomas, do you have anything to say?"

Thomas responded, "I quit."

The superior frowned and said, "I'm not surprised. You've done nothing but complain since you got here."

Hopefully you enjoyed that little joke. I shared it because it conveys an important truth: nothing more clearly indicates that we have succumbed to the devil than the words that come out of our mouths. When we complain about our lot in life, when we allow our conversation to be filled with whining and self-pity, we violate an important biblical principle I mentioned in an earlier chapter: never speak words that allow the enemy to think he's winning.

Again and again the Word of God shows that the mark of a mature Christian is that he rejoices in everything and gives thanks at all times. This does not mean God expects you to enjoy every circumstance in your life, nor does it mean that you should pretend to be happy in all things and force yourself to smile and put on a superficial attitude amidst your difficulties. But instead of adopting a fretful, whining attitude that fills your mouth with defeat and worry, the Bible says that you are to, "Put on the whole armor of God, that you may be able to stand against the wiles of the devil" (Eph. 6:11). I'll explain more about this in chapter 14. There's no other way to handle the devil's attacks.

One of the greatest weapons you have to combat the enemy of your soul is your mouth. Your words are what determine victory or defeat in many spiritual battles.

When Satan attacked a God-fearing man named Job in the

Old Testament, he was after one thing: Job's words. Notice in Job 1, Satan told God if he could be allowed to attack Job, he could get him to curse God. When the satanic attack blasted Job's life, he had to decide whether to curse God and die or bless God and live.

Never speak words that allow the enemy to think he's winning.

You must decide what comes out of your mouth when you are engaged in the onslaughts of hell. Will you curse God and die or bless God and live?

The python wants to choke your breath, silence your voice, and stop your witness. There is nothing that brings defeat to the enemy more than a child of God who learns to rejoice in the good times and the bad times.

You Have Something to Say!

Jesus explained, "Whoever says to this mountain, 'Be removed and be cast into the sea,' and does not doubt in his heart, but believes that those things he says will be done, he will have whatever he says" (Mark 11:23).

You and I are empowered to speak to mountains! When I think about what Jesus promised those who would believe Him and take Him at His Word, I think of the prophecy in Zechariah 4:6–7:

> This is the word of the LORD to Zerubbabel: "Not by might nor by power, but by My Spirit," says the LORD of hosts. "Who are you, O great mountain? Before Zerubbabel you shall become a plane! And he shall

bring forth the capstone with shouts of 'Grace, grace to it!'"

I quote Zechariah 4:6 a few times in this book because it's so powerful, but when you look at verse 7, it's even more incredible. God said that Zerubbabel had something to *say* to the mountain and it would become flattened. What mountains are in your way? Jesus made some very specific promises about mountain-moving faith. They are waiting on the sound of your voice.

There are times when we are called to pray corporately as a church, as believers, as a nation. It is powerful. Faith is released that can bring great victories, and we all benefit. At times you may be confronted with great difficulties, and God will send a comforting friend to stand with you and pray.

That is why Scripture says, "Strengthen the weak hands, and make firm the feeble knees" (Isa. 35:3). When one suffers, the body responds. When you are down, there is nothing at all wrong with calling somebody to say, "Pray for me because I'm really struggling right now." We all benefit by others' prayers. But there are mountains in your life that will only respond to *your voice.*

When Jesus talked about believing, He talked about it being a personal thing. That is why He made statements like, "All things are possible to him who believes" (Mark 9:23). He told the blind men as He healed them, "According to your faith let it be to you" (Matt. 9:29).

Your mountain knows your voice, and it will not move out of your life until you open your mouth and use your voice and your faith to change it. The preacher can lay hands on you, but that alone is not going to move your mountain. Others can pray for you, and it will encourage you and hopefully get you to a point where you will muster up enough faith to speak.

What do these mountains look like? One mountain people face is a behavioral mountain. Bad behavior patterns keep you from moving into the plans God has for you. Paul had a behavioral mountain in his life. He said, "For what I want to do I do not do, but what I hate I do" (Rom. 7:15, NIV). That was a major mountain of wrong behavior that was established in his life.

Are there behavioral issues that keep you tripped up? People encourage you to change, but nothing changes. You just keep doing the same old things. That mountain is never going to move until you put your faith where your mouth is and speak to that situation. Nobody can change your behavior for you—not even God! When you speak in faith, wanting that mountain to move and believing God will back your faith, it will crumble.

Financial mountains can seem totally impossible. They can be related to behavioral mountains, in that they often build up due to bad spending patterns. It seems like no matter how hard you try, you just cannot get on track financially. People can help you. God can bless you. But until you are ready to speak to that mountain and see it removed, it will continue to stand in your way.

It doesn't do any good to say, "Somebody needs to help me! Somebody needs to bail me out! Somebody needs to do something!" God is waiting for *you* to do something. At some point you have to take ownership and say, "My mountain only responds to my voice! And it is time for me to speak to this mountain of debt, get organized, follow a budget, and get it straightened out."

Let's not forget about the emotional mountains that sabotage success. These can develop from things like fear, anxiety, anger, or insecurity. People who face emotional mountains have difficulty accepting the love of God.

The enemy may be strangling you with emotional mountains of jealousy, fear, hurt, or abandonment. Those mountains will not go away until you open your mouth and say, "I will not be insecure. I will not be unloving. I will not be jealous. I will not be an angry person. I will not be a bitter person. I choose to let the love of God change my heart and flatten these mountains!" Whatever the situation may be, let your voice be heard.

The devil with his python ways wants to choke out your breath and keep you from speaking to the mountains in your life so that you stay defeated. And of course he also uses the massive relational mountains that can stand in your way.

Staying tangled in toxic, abusive, or destructive relationships can steal years from your life. You can go through counseling and therapy, but that mountain of wrong relationships is never going to get out of your life until you open your mouth. Your mountain knows your voice.

The supernatural power of the Word summons our faith. The Word of God can cause faith to be awakened and summoned in your life to your specific battlefield. You can overcome every obstacle if you will practice believing God's Word and pray out of that place of faith.

Python's influence tries to keep you bound and cut off prayer in your life. The longer it remains, the more it seems that you will never break free. It tries to keep you defeated and keep your goals out of reach. Over time it will make your mountain seem so big and permanent that instead of faith, you start operating in fear that your circumstances will never change.

BREAK FREE FROM THE PERMANENCY
AND PAIN OF YOUR MOUNTAINS

Jesus often pointed out His awareness of how long a person was in need of deliverance. Notice that He asked the father of the demon-possessed boy, "How long has this been happening to him?" (Mark 9:21). He asked the Pharisees who challenged Him for healing on the Sabbath, "Should not this woman, a daughter of Abraham, whom Satan has kept bound for eighteen long years, be set free on the Sabbath day from what bound her?" (Luke 13:16, NIV). Notice He said, "Eighteen *long* years." Jesus understands the feeling of desperation that can squeeze the life and hope out of us.

Why is this important? Because I believe it can free you from two things. First, it can free you from the power of permanency. A mountain speaks of permanency. Mountains represent things that are so big, and things that have been limiting your life for so long, that the enemy wants you to think they are permanent!

When you believe that, those mountains will always be there to keep you down and keep you from walking fully in the blessings and joy of God's will for your life. Faith can free you from things that the enemy says are permanent in your life. Carnal, temporal things will change. That is why Paul plainly stated, "So we fix our eyes not on what is seen, but on what is unseen. For what is seen is temporary, but what is unseen is eternal" (2 Cor. 4:18, NIV). The enemy wants you to think that anything you can see is permanent, but he is a liar! Jesus asked people, "How long?", because He wanted to break the power of permanency from their thoughts.

The enemy wants you to think that if you've dealt with something for years, you just have to accept it. "This marriage has always been like this." "My finances have always been like this." "My emotional dilemma has always been like this." The enemy wants you to think that you just have to accept it and you will never be able to change it or shake it off. But Jesus tells us if we will have faith in God, we can speak to that which seems permanent, and even though it looks like a mountain that's established and fixed, if we speak *faith*, it will be removed.

The second thing you can be free from is the power of pain. Doesn't pain have a way of just neutralizing us? You can pull one little muscle in your back, and your entire body wants to just sit down and avoid feeling that pain with every move. Not only that, but also every time you do move and that sharp pain shoots across your back, you're reminded of that weird move you made that caused the injury in the first place.

You sprain your ankle playing basketball, and every step reminds you of that layup you were going for and how you came down wrong on your ankle. You put ice on it. You elevate it. You go to sleep and forget all about it. The next morning your feet hit the floor, and as soon as you put weight on that ankle, the pain reminds you of what happened. That pain serves to take you right back to that place where you were hurt.

The same thing happens emotionally. You can suffer a wrong, an abuse, a hurt, and the enemy keeps jabbing at that pain in your heart to keep you limited. He connects pain to the memory to neutralize you. Every time you start to make progress, the enemy locks you back down into that pain, and then it connects you back to the past.

As long as the pain is there, you are still trapped by the memory. It winds around you like that python, slowly restricting and squeezing the life out of you. The enemy wants to keep you hurt over some situation, because as long as he has the pain that's still there, he can take you right back to that place even if it happened years ago.

It is crucial to speak in faith to your mountain in order to break the permanence and break the pain and say, "In the name of Jesus, I'm trading my sorrows in for the joy of the Lord." Jesus can heal the pain and cut through the cords of yesterday's painful memories. It has been long enough. It is time to break out of the devil's prison.

When you see a bound person, you are looking at an oppressed person. After fasting for forty days and being tempted by the devil in the desert, Jesus "returned in the power of the Holy Spirit," according to Luke 4:14. Then He explained that He was anointed:

> To preach the gospel to the poor; He has sent me to heal the brokenhearted, to proclaim liberty to the captives and recovery of sight to the blind, to set at liberty those who are oppressed.
>
> —LUKE 4:18

The King James translates the last line, "To set at liberty them that are *bruised*." Someone who is bound and oppressed is bruised in his or her soul. That is why so many stay bound to drugs and alcohol—because it numbs the pain. The enemy uses the pain to keep them bound and make them feel like a victim rather than a victor.

But Jesus has given us the power of victory. If you are bound, you need liberty. If the enemy has wrapped himself around your life, encircling you in your pain, you need the healing of the Lord. Do not allow the enemy to wrap around your future, your freedom, or your success.

I know that some people reading this book have been abused.

I know that some of you have gone through accidents, earth-shaking tragedies, or other terrible experiences. I'm not trying to minimize anything that has happened to you or the pain it has caused. But after a while you have to decide, "I don't want to be a victim anymore."

I like to say, "You just have to get a big, old 'So what?' down in your spirit." So what if they left you? Jesus will never leave you or forsake you. So what if they hurt you? Jesus is your healer. So what if that event stole from you and altered the course of your life and abilities? Through Jesus you can do all things! It's time to talk to the mountain and command it to get out of your life.

God said Zerubbabel would flatten the mountain in front of him with shouts of, "Grace to it!" (Zech. 4:7). *Grace* in that text means "highly favored." When you get a mountain in your life and it seems too big, it seems permanent, or it represents a painful past, the best thing you can do is look at that mountain and say, "I am highly favored."

- Mountain of discouragement: I am highly favored!

- Mountain of debt: I am highly favored!

- Mountain of fear: I am highly favored!

Try it. Use your voice to speak God's Word and grow your faith. You will not move the mountain by excavating it with your own strength. That's why the first part of that prophecy for Zerubbabel reads, "'Not by might nor by power, but by My Spirit,' says the LORD" (v. 6). You can only move the mountain if you have faith in God and you raise your voice against it.

Your voice can move mountains and activate angels. God

has angels assigned to you. They are ready and waiting to be dispatched at the sound of your voice.

In fact, I believe the greatest tragedy of prayerlessness is the unemployment of angels. Jesus prayed, and the angels came to Him in the garden; Paul prayed in a storm, and the angels came to him in a ship; the church prayed for Peter, and an angel delivered him and set him free. I wonder how many of the angels assigned to our lives are constantly standing in the unemployment line because we don't pray.

PRAYING TO BRING HIS PRESENCE

Reaching the presence of the Lord is the ultimate goal of raising your voice in prayer. Does your prayer life usher in God's presence in your home? Do you take God's presence home with you from church every Sunday, keeping God with you through prayer each day?

King David decided to bring God's presence home by moving the ark of the covenant, but he made the mistake of disrupting God's plan on how the ark should be moved. The whole story is found in 1 Chronicles 13:9–14, but I'll give you a summary.

The ark was always to be carried upon the shoulders of men, but they decided to load it on an ox-drawn cart instead. When one of the oxen stumbled and the ark tipped to one side as if it were about to tumble off of the cart, one of David's men, named Uzza, put his hand on the ark to stabilize it. This angered the Lord, and Uzza was immediately struck dead.

I imagine that shook the whole army, but it especially upset and frightened David. He decided not to bring the ark, the presence of God, home. Instead, he left it at the home of a humble man named Obed-Edom. Scripture says that, "The ark of God remained with the family of Obed-Edom in his house three months. And the LORD blessed the house of Obed-Edom and all that he had" (v. 14).

We see the same problems today. Perhaps we experience the glorious presence of God in our church, but what good does it do if we leave the presence there and go right back to our homes without carrying the presence home with us? I am convinced we are not taking God's presence home. I am convinced that we go to church and get happy, blessed, and excited and then go home and let hell rule our family life.

Something is wrong, because whatever happens in the house of God should happen in your house. You cannot cut God off. You cannot come to church on Sunday and then say "That was good, God, I enjoyed being in Your presence," and then exclude Him from your thoughts the rest of the week. When you live like the devil all week long—that is whose presence you will have. One dose of God on Sunday will not carry you through.

I believe God is saying, "It is time for you to take Me home. I want to be in your house. I want to bless you and all that you have. I want to be in your marriage, on your job, on that plane with you, and in that car with you. I do not want you to leave My presence and cut Me off from your personal life; I want you to receive blessings at home. I want to visit you in intimate ways when you are alone."

As I said earlier in this chapter, a whole generation has been raised up that does not bring Him home. We come to church, and our children think we are schizophrenic because we cuss, fuss, and scream at home and in the car, then smile, clap, and raise our hands and our voices in praise at church.

It is not pleasing to the Lord for hell to go on in your home all week only to have you bring out your church attitude as you enter the church building. Is there not more to being a

Christian than to come to church once a week on Sunday and then go home to an empty prayer life? Not having a diligent prayer life leaves your home open for attack.

I am convinced that we go to church and get happy, blessed, and excited and then go home and let hell rule our family life.

Obed-Edom was not a king. He was not a mighty man. In fact, he was not even a soldier. He was a nobody. He does not appear in the Bible until this occasion. But when he saw that the king did not want God's presence in his home, he said, "I'll take it," and the Bible states that the ark of the covenant was placed in his care.

I researched the name Obed-Edom and found that one of its meanings is *worshipper*. If you desire to maintain the presence of God in your home, a certain attitude must be a part of maintaining it. I believe worship and prayer were constant in Obed-Edom's house. There was no devilish python slithering in to steal and destroy.

Why can't we do this in our homes? We get excited, but we do not have the discipline to go home and set up family devotions. We are so busy. Obed-Edom had to rearrange his priorities. He had to be the high priest in his home and take control of what took place in his home if he wanted God's presence to remain.

Obed-Edom had eight sons, and not one of them was backslidden, not one was on drugs, not one was in prison or living in sin. The Bible says all eight of them were mighty men of valor.

If we bring the presence of God home, our children and our marriage will be affected. If we bring it home, we will not speak negatively, scream, holler, fuss, fight, criticize one another, or cut each other down. Instead, the atmosphere of our lives will be changed, and peace and contentment will prevail rather than a battle zone.

The problem is that many are not willing to make the necessary sacrifices so that God's presence will be the central focus of their homes. Your home will either be filled with God or filled with the enemy. God will not remain where the enemy is invited and made comfortable. Without prayer, snakes will enter your house.

God requires holiness and purity in our lives. If you want to be part of a move of God, you cannot live like the devil. You must remain holy and pure—and you must be ready to praise God in all circumstances of your life.

eight

STOPPING YOUR PRAISE

AUL AND SILAS faced an unexpected turn of events after they cast the spirit of Python out of the young slave girl. She used her demonically inspired talents to make a pretty good income for her slave masters. Like modern-day pimps, they sat back and collected money while she did the work. When her masters saw that she no longer had "the gift," they became infuriated. They went looking for Paul and Silas and "dragged them into the marketplace to the authorities" (Acts 16:19).

Notice that they didn't tell the judge, "These men cast a powerful demonic influence out of our slave girl and now we can't rip people off any longer." Instead, they suddenly became very pious and civically minded. They claimed, "These men, being Jews, exceedingly trouble our city; and they teach customs which are not lawful for us, being Romans, to receive or observe" (vv. 20–21).

Keep in mind, Paul was a Jew *and* he was a Roman citizen. However, the lies the two men told incited the crowd. Outraged, they most likely stripped Paul and Silas for further humiliation, and then beat and whipped them publicly. Finally, they threw them into prison. The jailer put them in "the inner prison" for fear of the crowd and magistrates, and they chained their feet in stocks.

What a day! Paul and Silas were on their way to prayer. The spirit of Python rose up to stop them. They cast it out. They get judged publicly, beaten severely, and thrown into prison. They were put into the deepest section and chained with heavy stocks.

I can imagine them both starting to regain consciousness hours later on that damp prison floor. They slowly pulled themselves upright, no doubt with some groaning and wincing as a few broken ribs, cuts, and bruises reminded them of the day's events. Their eyes adjusted to the darkness enough to see a few rats running around, and the unmistakable smell of sewage filled their nostrils.

Paul and Silas could have started complaining about their unfair treatment and untended wounds. But they did not. They could have complained to God that they were treated so harshly for pursuing His call to spread the gospel. But they did not.

Those two bleeding, hurting men simply lifted up their voices and started praying and praising God. Though they should have been asleep, the other prisoners quietly listened to their song.

It must have been such a sweet sound to the Lord's ears. It was a sound the enemy hoped to choke out, but praise breaks the grip of the enemy and changes the atmosphere. It invites the presence of God into your circumstances.

That little Macedonian prison cell was just too small to contain His presence. Around midnight, as Paul and Silas continued to sing, the walls of the prison began to tremble. The floor began to shake. Stones fell. Mortar crumbled. Chains broke free. Hinges fell out of their place. "Suddenly there was a great earthquake, so that the foundations of the prison were shaken; and immediately all the doors were opened and everyone's chains were loosed" (Acts 16:26).

The prison guard was awakened by the ruckus. Thinking that all the prisoners escaped during his watch, he was seriously contemplating suicide. But Paul let him know that not one prisoner was missing.

A lot of people enjoy praising God in the sunshine, but what about in the darkness of a prison cell? Is God only worth praising when we feel that He has "come through" for us? Is He only worthy to be praised when we are blessed financially and everything is going our way?

David wrote, "Every day I will bless You, and I will praise Your name forever and ever. Great is the LORD, and greatly to be praised; and His greatness is unsearchable. One generation shall praise Your works to another, and shall declare Your mighty acts" (Ps. 145:2–4).

He is worthy of praise *every day*—not just on good days. We need to know how to praise Him in the darkness of midnight—perhaps more than *any* other time. Praise changes the atmosphere and welcomes the presence of God.

No Worship, No Rain

One of the greatest lessons the Lord ever taught me about worship is found in the Book of Zechariah, chapter 14. It changed my life. "And it shall be that whichever of the families of the earth do not come up to Jerusalem to worship the King, the LORD of hosts, on them there will be no rain" (v. 17). No worship, no rain; plain and simple.

The reason this verse is such a great revelation about worship is because rain is often symbolic of the outpouring of the

Holy Spirit. Praise is like a cloud that forms in the atmosphere. Once enough of it accumulates, it drops rain.

You are called to be a rainmaker. Our churches need rain. Our families need rain. Our neighborhoods, cities, and states need rain. Our country desperately needs the rain of the Holy Spirit—and that will only happen when prayer and praise change the atmosphere.

> Is God only worth praising when we feel that He has "come through" for us? Is He only worthy to be praised when we are blessed financially and everything is going our way?

If worship services at your church are cold, dry, and lifeless— kick in and get your praise on. Don't just fit in and conform. Get a smile on your face. Get some energy in your song. Sing not just for people but for the King of glory Himself.

Psalm 150:6 says everything that has breath should praise the Lord. If you have breath, you are to praise the Lord. Remember that a python is out to squeeze the breath out of its victims. He is out to stop praise.

WAYS TO PRAISE

There are many expressions of praise in the Bible. One is simply the lifting of your hands (Ps. 134:2). I believe lifting your hands is a unique expression of praise because your fingerprints distinguish you from everyone else. When you raise them to God, I believe you are reaching out and touching Him in a way that symbolizes your unique individual relationship with Him.

We praise Him with musical instruments as Psalm 150 declares. David was a warrior, but he was first and foremost *a worshipper.* He played music and sang praises to the Lord since his childhood. His praise was a powerful weapon against the enemy. When David played his harp for King Saul, the "distressing spirit" that tormented him would be subdued (1 Sam. 16:23).

Every time you pluck a guitar, hit a chord, beat a drum, or crash a cymbal in praise to God, you send demons fleeing. If it is with a heart submitted to God, a heart of worship, then you are not just playing music. You are making rain.

Scripture tells us to clap our hands and shout to God (Ps. 47:1). A shout can change the dry atmosphere. I have been in many services when the songs of praise were going just so high. Then someone full of praise shouts out, "Hallelujah! Praise the Lord!", and the whole place breaks loose with shouts and songs of praise.

You can praise the Lord through dance (Ps. 150:4), leaping, bowing down before Him, and even by standing to your feet in honor of His presence. Whichever way you choose to praise Him, your praise changes the atmosphere and breaks the grip of the enemy off of your life because it strengthens your relationship with the Father.

However, if nothing goes up, nothing comes down. No worship, no rain. That's why the python wants to keep the atmosphere dry and to choke the life out of your praise.

WHY WE PRAISE

In 2 Chronicles chapter 20 we find a large army coming to make war against Jehoshaphat. When he received the news, Jehoshaphat and the people of Judah sought the Lord through fasting and prayer. Everyone gathered, and He prayed in their presence, seeking help from God and waiting upon Him. They bowed in worship before the Lord and began to sing and praise

Him loudly. They were making rain. The next day Jehoshaphat put the praisers and worshippers in *front* of the army! When the enemy armies heard the praise, they turned on each other and destroyed themselves.

This shows us the power of praise. It is connected to the victory Jesus has won over the python and everything the enemy has put in motion against you.

Praise is not based on your circumstances. It is based on who He is. Paul and Silas were not just "sunshine praisers," worshipping God only when things were going well. They were midnight, dirty-dungeon praisers as well.

Paul didn't have a lot going for him physically. He probably did not have the greatest voice either. God is not as interested in talent as He is in character. We are into showboats, but God would rather have someone who will praise Him out of pain. He loves it when someone who is in his or her midnight hour still has praise.

Constant private worship equals powerful public worship. You do not walk out and celebrate publicly what you have not celebrated privately. The greater your private worship, the greater your public ministry will be. What you do all week in private will determine your anointing in public.

When praise is locked up by the python, revival is locked up, breakthrough is locked up, and victory is locked up. What does the enemy use to keep you from praising God? Is it murmuring, complaining, negative talk, or faultfinding? You are never going to experience victory while you're talking defeat.

If Paul and Silas decided to sit around in that cell focusing on how they were mistreated, how they felt defeated, or how they would get even with those who beat them, they would have rotted there.

The Best Kind of Praise

God looks for praise that is borne out of our times of adversity or affliction. Sometimes He leads us into experiences that are unpleasant, difficult, or even painful. His Word says that He tests us in the furnace of affliction (Isa. 48:10).

I don't know why, but there are times when God allows every one of us to go through a furnace of affliction. There is a particular sound of worship that can only come from one who has gone through trials.

Maybe there has been a fiery furnace in your health, your marriage, or regarding a family member. That python, Satan, wants to coil around your situation and twist the purposes of God to make you feel abandoned and forgotten. He knows that when you lose hope, you lose praise.

What you do all week in private will determine your anointing in public.

Do not be deceived by the liar. Set your heart on the God who is faithful, who loves you, who has called you and equipped you to overcome. The heart after God finds a way to praise Him, even in the heat of the trial.

If you have breath, you can praise the Lord. You may not have a job, but you have breath. You may not have a car, but you have breath.

As I said earlier in this chapter, there are many ways to praise the Lord—with lifted hands, dancing feet, and bowed bodies. But there is a praise that needs nothing but your breath. It is a praise that rises out of the furnace where you have lost everything *but* your breath. It is a praise that is not attached to material possessions or specific happenings. It is a praise that comes when you praise God in spite of it all.

When you go through the fire, you can see what you really have inside. Determine that as long as you have breath, you will praise Him.

Sometime ago I read a story about a fire that started in South Bend, Indiana, in a computer store. The local fire department was first on the scene. They hosed the outside of the building, but it was having little effect on the fire inside.

As the fire continued to spread and become more intense, they sent out a call for assistance from other fire companies. One of the smaller departments from a neighboring county rushed to help.

They had a small budget, and their fire truck was old. When they arrived at full speed, they went right over the curb, across the yard, and right through the wall of the building into the fire. While they were in there, they pulled their water hoses out and went to work. They managed to put out the fire that couldn't be handled before. They were able to do more from the inside than the other fire company could do from the outside.

The next day the owner of the business offered that little fire company a check for ten thousand dollars in appreciation for the bravery they showed by driving right into the middle of the fire. When the press asked the fire chief what he would use the money for, he told them the first thing they would do is buy some new brakes for their truck!

Those firemen never planned to go straight into the middle of the fire. Maybe you didn't plan to be where you are right now. God wants you to know that He has you there because there are things you can do from the inside of that fiery situation better than you can do from the outside. You can't tell how powerful your faith is until you've been into the fire. God wants to unlock your praise. It can be your response no matter what you face.

Did you ever play on the playground when you were young? When I was a kid, we had team captains. They were always the bigger, stronger guys, and they would divide up the rest of us one by one as they chose team members. It could be kind of embarrassing if you were a little guy like me. I would just be standing there thinking, "Please, God, don't let me be the last."

There's always somebody who is picked last, someone who doesn't seem qualified to be on the team. God says, "What qualifies you for My team is the furnace." If you are in a furnace, it is an indication that God has an assignment for you.

- David was chosen out of the fire. He said we will have troubles. but God will deliver us out of them all (Ps. 34:19). David did not deny that trouble existed in life, but he knew God was the deliverer no matter what happened.

- Job was chosen out of the fire. He was determined to serve God no matter what: "Though He slay me, yet will I trust Him" (Job 13:15). Job lost his children, his livelihood, his wealth, his health—everything. He had nothing left but his breath. In the middle of it all Job praised God. That is why God chose him. Through all he had endured, Job was able to boldly say, "When He has tested me, I shall come forth as gold" (Job 23:10).

- Joseph was chosen out of the fire. He was despised by his own family, rejected, tempted, lied about, falsely accused, and punished for a crime he did not commit. Yet in the end Joseph knew that what men meant for evil, God would use for good. God chose him out of the fire, put him in a palace, and used him to save a generation.

Ultimately the furnace of adversity does not *make* you; it *reveals* you. The fire shows what you really are on the inside. You can lose your praise or find it during a fiery trial.

"Add a Verse" Through Adversity

I like to tell people that adversity "adds a verse" to your life. In a song the verses change while the chorus stays the same. Whatever you are going through, you can let it subtract from your life or add another verse to it. Just remember, "God adds a verse to me through adversity." Those verses add to your life-long song of praise and worship that is priceless to Him.

When you first get saved, you know Him as Savior. When you get sick, you find out a new "verse" as you come to know Him as healer. When you suffer loss, you discover Him as comforter. When you have financial troubles, you know Him as a provider. When your children are in trouble, you find out He is your protector. As you walk through life, you find that God keeps adding another verse to your song of praise. The chorus remains the same: "God's faithful." But the longer you live, the more verses you add.

A furnace of affliction will not kill you. It will not destroy you. It will add a new verse to your song of faith. You may see that python coiling around, trying to choke out your breath, trying to silence your voice. Lift up a praise to God and break free.

One place that you will encounter pure praise is on the mission field. When I visited Nigeria, the church there had no dramatic lighting, no sound system, and no air conditioning. The worship leader played a small, kid-sized keyboard that was barely big enough for his fingers. A guy playing half a drum set accompanied him. The two microphones had duct tape on them, and a guy held the plug in the wall throughout the service so it wouldn't fall out. Yet they were so full of joy, and there was such a tangible spirit of praise in that place.

> The furnace of adversity does not make you; it reveals you. The fire shows what you really are on the inside.

It is not about what you have or don't have. If it takes elaborate "bells and whistles" to get your praise going, you have likely never been through anything. But if you have ever been through a furnace of affliction, it produces praise in you even if you do not like the singer, the song, or the music. You just have to turn your praise loose. When praise goes up, rain comes down.

Paul and Silas were arrested for lifting up the name of Jesus. They were beaten and shackled. The officials could chain their bodies, but they could not chain their praise. As they praised God at midnight, an earthquake rattled the foundations of that prison, and their chains broke loose. Every prison door was opened.

When you unlock your praise, your praise will unlock you! What has you bound? What chains are restricting your life and ministry? Do not stop praising Him. Not only will it unlock your situation, but it will unlock the situations of others around you as well.

Any time you go through a severe furnace of affliction and you begin to praise God, it can set people free who are linked and connected to you. Out of the most painful experiences and traumas of your life, instead of internalizing and being depressed, you learn to transform the atmosphere with praise. Instead of becoming depressed, a tear of adoration and joy will come to your eye to know that God was so faithful and that He saw you through.

My prayer is that as you've read this chapter, you've decided that the enemy will no longer choke out your praise. In the next chapter we'll look at more of his python-like schemes to limit us as he tries to snuff out our spiritual life.

ninenine

LIMITING YOUR LIFE

T HE DEVIL WORKS like a python to restrict your growth and limit your influence. When a python is squeezing its prey, not only is the victim's breath stopped, but movement is also completely restricted. I see the enemy causing the same immobility in the lives of Christians. He puts limitations on our lives, and we accept them without a fight. In this chapter I'm going to show you several ways the python wants to put limitation in your life.

The spirit of limitation says, "I know that the blessings of God are real. I know that the Holy Spirit's power is real, that miracles are real, that healing is real, that prosperity is real. I know that it exists, but it's not for me." That's the python putting limitation on your life.

The python puts a ceiling over you that says, "You can go this far but no farther. You can have this much but no more. You can succeed to this degree, but you peaked, and you're not going any higher." That's the limiting spirit of the enemy.

If you're not careful, the python will slowly begin tightening his coils around your life, and you'll begin to accept those limitations. Then when the Holy Spirit says, "Come a little farther...do a little more...expand just a little bit," you won't have the faith to follow Him.

The limiting spirit likes to remind you of your past. But I

want to say, you're not the person you used to be. When Jesus came into your heart, you might have been anchored to an addiction or chained to alcohol or failure. Don't let those chains stop you or limit you!

Maybe he whispers in your ear, "Nobody in your family has ever had a successful marriage. You can't expect to have a good marriage that lasts for life. Don't you even think it."

Maybe when you go to church, the python wraps around you, and you sit back and can't clap or raise your hands. You can't even smile. This is one of the first ways to detect that you are in the grip of the python.

He can try to limit your giving too. You know how to break python's limitations off of your finances? Give more than you've ever given before! Be faithful to God. Honor the Lord with your tithe and your offerings. If you haven't been doing it, make the vow now, and God will bless you more and more and more and more, even in the middle of a bad economy.

The enemy wants you to stay defeated. The enemy wants you to put your head down. The enemy wants you to hide in a fox-hole because everything's rough. But the Lord has a remedy for those who have been limited: He wants to enlarge the place of your dwelling, and He wants you to believe Him for greater things.

I also want to point out that it's important what you say. Make sure you don't speak limitation over your life. The Bible says in Psalm 78 that "they limited the Holy One of Israel" when they said, "Can God spread a table in the wilderness [in this economy]?" Notice that the python's power of limitation in their lives increased when they said, "Can God." I like to say, "You are either a 'Can-Godder' or a 'God-Canner.'"

You need to quit asking "Can God" and start saying "God

can," because your words are multipliers. By that, I mean that whatever you say, you multiply in your life. Do you speak lack? Do you speak limitation? Do you speak recession? Do you speak bankruptcy? Do you speak disease? Do you speak fear? Do you speak defeat? Then guess what: you're multiplying that thing that you have spoken in your life. Your words are multipliers. The Bible says, "Death and life are in the power of the tongue" (Prov. 18:21).

Have you been saying "Can God" or "God *can*"? Begin declaring how big your God is today. "God *can* spread a table for me." "God *can* bless me in this economy." "God *can* free me from every limitation."

LET GO OF THE BAGGAGE

Another way python puts limitation in your life is by keeping you weighed down with baggage. We read in 1 Samuel that Saul was a tall, handsome young man from the tribe of Benjamin. One day his father, Kish, asked him to go with a servant to find some donkeys that had broken loose from their pen. They searched all day and night and could not find the donkeys. Saul wanted to give up. But the servant told him there was a prophet in the city who might be able to help. Saul and the servant decided to go to the gates of the city to ask the prophet if he knew where the donkeys might be.

While Saul and his servant were making their way toward the gates of the city, the Spirit of the Lord came upon the prophet Samuel, whom they were headed to see. The Lord told him to rise up and go to the gate, where he would meet the man he would anoint as the first king of Israel.

Samuel went to the gate and began to watch the people. The moment he laid eyes upon Saul, the Holy Spirit confirmed in his heart that Saul was the man. So Samuel introduced himself and invited Saul to eat with him and stay the night. The next morning they got up and went to the gate of the city to wait.

Keep in mind; Saul's life is about to change forever. But he still had his mind on those lost donkeys. We can miss what God has because we're chasing trivial things. Samuel told him, "Do not be anxious about them, for they have been found" (1 Sam. 9:20). Saul needed to wait on the Lord.

The enemy wants you to stay anxious. He wants to keep you occupied with trivial things—donkey chasing—instead of God chasing. But I believe the Lord has a word for everyone reading this book. I believe He wants you to know that the issues of life have already been handled by Him. You have no idea how God is about to use you and no idea how badly the enemy wants to limit you. God has amazing things planned for your life.

Don't get busy chasing donkeys and distracted by things that do not matter. You are headed for the throne. You are a king in the kingdom. The Lord wants you to know that there are many people who miss great opportunities because they are distracted chasing other things.

Your "donkey" might be a person, a mistake, a temptation, a job. There are always donkeys that will pull you away. If you allow them, they will rob you of your kingship. Don't let your baggage keep you from God's best.

Samuel anointed Saul at the gate and told him he would be king. A few months later the big day came when all of Israel gathered by the tens of thousands to crown Saul as the first king of Israel. The men were celebrating in the streets; the women were dancing with timbrels and tambourines; the children had streamers in their hands. It was a huge celebration. But there was one problem: Saul was nowhere to be found.

We've all seen that moment of anticipation when the trumpets sound and the name is announced, but all you can hear is crickets chirping. So they announce the name again, but still no one comes.

Since God had chosen him, they must have figured God knew Saul's whereabouts. "Therefore they inquired of the LORD further, 'Has the man come here yet?' And the LORD answered, 'There he is, hidden among the equipment'" (1 Sam. 10:22). The word *equipment* was originally the term for *baggage*. When the big day arrived, Saul was so weighed down with baggage that he could not step in to what God had called him to do. He was hiding.

This is one of the ways the enemy puts limitation on your life. He keeps you from receiving the blessings of God. You will miss the indescribable blessings of God if you don't let go of some baggage. Stop chasing "donkeys" that do not really matter in the big picture of God's plan for your life. Quit hiding and allowing baggage to hold you back from your calling. Baggage from the past will hinder you from moving into God's plan. He has something better waiting for you if you will just let go and trust Him. It is not about your strength or ability.

There comes a time in the life of every believer when you have to say, "I'm not staying here any longer! I'm not staying here in this episode that is killing me, draining me, and holding me back. It is time for me to get over it. I'm a king not a donkey chaser!" You have to make a decision not to be chained to it or defeated by it.

"Baggage" can come in the form of false teaching, from

lack of understanding, even from inside your own family. Old wives' tales do not replace the solid Word of God. Step out of that stuff. Leave the baggage behind.

NO MORE DUCT-TAPE FAITH!

The python will also try to put limitation on your life by sending a spirit of lack, a spirit that presses you down and says, "You will operate at this level for the rest of your life." And as long as you stay at that level, the enemy doesn't bother you, but just as soon as you start to lift your head up and say, "I'm going to another level so that I can do more for God, my family, and the kingdom," that spirit of lack will show up and try to keep you in that same territory. Sometimes the enemy holds folks in the same territory for generation after generation.

You will miss the indescribable blessings of God if you don't let go of some baggage. Quit allowing baggage to hold you back from your calling.

The spirit of lack isn't just about finances; it can be a lack of joy, lack of love in your marriage, lack of confidence, lack of peace, lack of health in your body, or many other things. It's very, very real, and if you don't watch it, you begin to develop a mentality that you receive from the spirit of lack that says, "Things will never change for me. God blesses others, but He'll never bless me, and I don't expect any more."

Listen, everybody goes through difficult times. Stop listening to the spirit of lack that says, "Keep your head down and stay oppressed, defeated, depressed, wanting everything, and barely getting by." That's what I call settling for "duct-tape faith."

Some of you may recognize this term "duct-tape faith" from a message I preached about the four horns of Zechariah 1:17–21. I also mention it in my book *Believe That You Can*. But for those who have never heard of duct-tape faith, let me explain what I'm talking about.

The duct-tape level is when you buy stuff on sale and then you return it at another store where it's not on sale and make a little bit of money. That's duct-tape level.

The duct-tape level is when you owe two bills and you don't have money for either one. So you "accidentally" put the check to pay for the gas bill in the envelope to the power company, and the check for the power company goes to the gas company to buy more time. I know some of you reading this know what I'm talking about!

Your faith is at duct-tape level when it doesn't even cross your mind to believe God for something better. You tell yourself, "Just keep holding things together. Just stretch these resources a little bit farther. We can't afford to fix it or replace it, so hurry and patch it up before it falls apart. Go get the duct tape!"

I got the idea of duct-tape faith at a time when our television ministry was struggling. I remember one day while I waited in our studio for them to set up so I could record an intro to an upcoming program. I looked around, and there was duct tape on everything. Duct tape held the lenses on the cameras. Duct tape held the wires together. Duct tape was holding the lights in place. Even the recorders they were using to make copies and send them out to different nations were all duct-taped together. Then I noticed our television director just carried around a big wad of duct tape with him everywhere he went.

As I looked around, the Lord spoke to me and said, "That's the kind of faith you've got: duct-tape faith." I remember it like it was yesterday. He said, "You know why you're at duct-tape level? Because you don't believe Me for anything better than this."

I determined right then and there to break loose from the duct-tape level! And when the cameras rolled that day I said, "Now listen. We're trying to build a sanctuary. We don't have enough money to build the sanctuary, and we certainly don't have enough to buy new equipment. That's why I've got duct tape all over everything. But in Jesus's name, I believe God has told me He is going to take the duct tape off of our ministry." The python and his spirit of lack wanted me to accept things as they were, but instead I made a declaration of what God had said to me.

Within thirty days more than a million dollars came in, and we bought the latest television equipment that money can buy. The spirit of lack wanted me to accept that duct-tape level. The spirit of lack said, "It'll never be any better," but I refused to believe it.

Are you under the grip of python in your life right now? Has he put a spirit of lack on your life? Are you settling for duct-tape faith? Are you always "robbing Peter to pay Paul," and you don't even think that God can bless you, prosper you, or increase you?

Sometimes when it seems like everything in life is failing, when everything you touch falls apart, it is hard to stay focused on the promises of God. It seems easier to put duct tape on your problems. With the weight of that python coiled around you, it becomes very inviting to just sit down and give up. "Just stop fighting it," he whispers. "Just stop breathing. Stop breathing in the Word. Stop breathing out a praise."

Instead of accepting that duct-tape level, why don't you just say, "In the name of Jesus, spirit of lack, it's not legal for you to be in my life. I serve a God of abundance. I serve a God of more than enough. I know what His Word has promised to me. I will praise Him in spite of my circumstances."

Don't listen to the voices on the news. Don't listen to the voice of the python that says your business is going under or your kids are never going to serve God or you'll never regain your health. I'm writing this book to tell you that you *can* expect God to come through! You can break the grip of python and that spirit of limitation and tell it to get out of your life in Jesus's name. You can conquer the very thing that is out to conquer you.

God has made provision for your victory and success in life. "But thank God! He gives us victory over sin and death through our Lord Jesus Christ" (1 Cor. 15:57, NLT). Do not let the enemy prohibit your growth. Don't allow your present circumstances to limit your faith or dictate your future. Temporary circumstances can feel like a permanent future when we are under severe attack. When those coils of python wrap around, your breath gets weaker, and it feels like hope is lost. Just like those "snake eggs" I talked about in chapter 4, that spirit of lack can get in your head and spread negativity, discouragement, and hopelessness.

It can slip into your marriage. I like to joke that when you first start out in married life, everything is wonderful. Married life starts out *ideal*. A few months later there's an *ordeal*, and before long you're thinking, "This is a *raw deal*." Then you start looking for a *new deal* because a spirit of lack has come into your marriage.

All joking aside, no matter what seems to be going wrong in your life, God is not through with you. I know people are dealing with increasingly difficult things in the world and in their individual lives. Some even ask, "If God is with me, why does He let these things happen to me?"

I'm going to say something that might surprise you: God being with you has nothing to do with having a perfect life. Life in general is a battle. However, when God is with you, you are no longer fighting the battle of life in your own limited strength, but in His unlimited strength.

God wants to take you to a new level beyond duct-tape faith. You just have to trust Him to carry you through. Press in to His presence and trust Him, even in difficult times. He *will* come through for you.

GETTING PAST BIG

It's easy to see how the python limits us when things are tough, but did you know he also works very slyly to put limitations on us in successful times as well? It starts with what we think of as "big." There's a magical measurement in each person's mind that defines big for them. Right now as you read this, I'm sure you can think of what big means to you. If I say, "Big money," "Big church," or "Big success," you have an idea in your mind of what those things look like.

To break free from the python's limitations, you have to get past the thing in your mind that you perceive as big and redefine big according to God's definition. If you don't, the python will easily be able to put limitations on your life.

I know what I'm talking about because in every level of

ministry that I've experienced, at some point in my mind I've had to get past what I thought was big. When I was growing up, my dad never pastored big, big churches. So in my mind, when Free Chapel hit seven hundred people, I thought, "Whoa, this is big!" Looking back on it now, I can see that the church stayed at that level for a while because I was accepting the limitations the enemy had put on my faith. Python and his sly, sneaky limiting spirit really messed with me at that point.

I'm going to say something that might surprise you: God being with you has nothing to do with having a perfect life.

I recently found an old newsletter I had written in 1993. I had said, "We really need to pray. We're starting our first twenty-one-day fast. Here's what we're fasting for. We've got three hundred fifty empty seats in the new sanctuary."

This shows that I was struggling with having enough faith for what I considered to be big. I didn't know if we'd ever get those seats filled. I remember there were three whole sections in the balcony, and they drove me batty. Why? I had a limited idea of what big meant, and to me, filling those three hundred fifty seats was beyond big.

God finally broke through that limiting spirit by building up my faith through His Word, through prophecies, and through times of prayer. Then we moved into a new building, and I thought, "This is big!" Then it filled up. Then we added the California campus, and it filled up. Now we have a third campus, and it is filling up.

Every time I've thought "This is big," God has caused my faith to go up another notch. I've had to push against that python grip on my faith, my dreams, and my vision. When my faith saw it done, it happened.

You have to push against the limitations of the enemy. That's why I talk about building and expanding the ministry all the time. I know some people look at me like I'm crazy, but I'm dealing with the spirit of limitation. I'm dealing with the spirit of lack. I am exercising my faith to get past what I think is big, to break free from the python's hold on my life and ministry.

I challenge you today to look with eyes of faith, see beyond the limits of what you think is big for your life—your marriage, your family, your business, your career, your finances, your health, your ministry—and begin to declare things like, "Expand! Enlarge! Increase!"

God says, "When your faith is ready, I'm ready." So push against that limitation. No more duct tape! No more scraping by! No more fixing up! No limits. It's time for a new harvest to come. Break off the python grip over your life that is limiting you. Push past what you think is big. God wants to enlarge your territory. He wants to increase you and prosper you so that you can increase His kingdom.

YOUR "SECOND WHEN"

You have probably heard the expression "to catch your second wind," meaning to renew strength after exerting yourself at something. However, you may not know about catching your "second when."

Paul wrote to the Corinthians, "*When* I was a child, I spoke as a child, I understood as a child, I thought as a child; but *when* I became a man, I put away childish things" (1 Cor. 13:11, emphasis added). There are two spiritual seasons in our lives that I call "whens."

The first "when" is being born again into God's family. When you first accept the Lord as your Savior, you enter a childhood stage. You grow in your relationship with God by reading and studying His Word and talking to Him in prayer. You learn from teachers of His Word how to walk and live by faith. You learn about real love, peace, and purity. You begin to learn His ways.

At some point you hit your second "when," which is adulthood. As a mature Christian you begin to witness Jesus's love and what He's done for you, and you begin to lead others to Him.

The problem is, many people never get past childhood because they can't overcome their past. This is yet another way the python brings limitation into our lives. We are not supposed to get stuck in childish, carnal ways. We were meant to grow as a seed in the ground and to produce and reproduce after our kind the likeness of God in us.

We are supposed to change year to year in our relationship with Jesus, in our love walk, and in our worship and prayer time. Growing people are changing people.

The Lord gave me a simple thought through Paul's words. Catching your second "when" requires sanctification. The theme of this whole text is change. There is the "when" of childhood, and then secondly, there's the "when" of adulthood, but a lot of people are trapped in "protracted childhood." They can't seem to break out.

Maybe you've been born again and gotten into the kingdom, but you seem to be trapped. You must somehow move beyond the first "when" and catch your second "when." Many people settle for the mediocre, just being in the kingdom. There is a second move that God wants to do.

The enemy would like to convince you that you will never get past the past. You can't change the past, but you don't have to remain there. There's nothing Satan likes better than to get a believer started on a guilt trip. You can't change the mistakes or failures of the past. What you *can* do is close the book on your past and know that God has a second "when" for you. You don't have to live still bound in the prison of whatever happened. If Satan keeps reminding you of your past, it's because he's running out of new material!

One of the most successful tactics demons use in neutralizing Christians is to get them to dwell on all their failures. Once they begin feeling guilty about their performance in the Christian life, they will no longer be any threat to Satan's program.

One of Satan's greatest ploys is to blind us to the cross. I want to say something loud and clear: "He has now reconciled you in His fleshly body through death, in order to present you before Him holy and blameless and beyond reproach" (Col. 1:22, NAS).

In Isaiah 43:25 God says "I, even I, am he who blots out your transgressions, for my own sake, and remembers your sins no more" (NIV). God can't even remember your sins, so stop trying to remind Him of what He's trying to forget. Satan does not want you to remember that God did away with your sin at the cross. It's time to agree with God and see yourself as God sees you. There's a passage in Colossians 2:14 that thrills me every time I read it: "Having canceled out the certificate of debt, consisting of decrees against us, which was hostile to us; and He has taken it out of the way, having nailed it to the cross" (NAS).

What a beautiful word picture. Whenever a person would be convicted in a Roman court, a certificate of debt would be prepared. It was a list of every crime the person was accused of committing. It would then be taken with the prisoner to wherever he would be imprisoned and nailed to the door of the cell. What an illustration the apostle Paul used to show how God dealt with our sins.

If Satan keeps reminding you of your past, it's because he's running out of new material!

When Jesus hung on the cross two thousand years ago, the certificate of debt of every person who would ever live was nailed to the cross with Him. Our certificate of debt listed every sin. Just as the certificate would have been nailed to the cell of the criminal, Jesus took our certificate of debt and nailed it to the cross. Why? To pay the debt of our sin.

According to Roman law, when a person was put in prison and the certificate of debt was nailed to the door, it would remain there until the sentence was carried out. Then they would take the certificate and write across it the word meaning "IT IS FINISHED." They would roll it up and give it to the prisoner, and he could never be punished for those crimes again.

Just before Jesus bowed His head and said, "Father, into your hands I commit My spirit," He gave a victory cry and said, "It is finished!" (John 19:30). The Greek word for this is *teleo*, meaning "paid in full." Jesus took our certificate of debt and wrote across it with His own blood, "It is finished," paid in full.

We can never be tried for our sins again after we've received His pardon. That's why Colossians 2:14 says He has taken away our certificate of debt, "having nailed it to the cross." That's why Christ died on the cross. He took care of our sin problem forever. Now God wants us to serve Him not out of duty but out of thanksgiving for what He has done through Jesus Christ.

Hebrews 9:14 says, "How much more shall the blood of Christ...cleanse your conscience from dead works to serve the living God?" Let the blood of Jesus Christ cleanse your conscience from the guilt of sin. Then walk in the new authority and understand who you are in Christ.

Too many people have been in church for years but are still in the "childhood" stage. That is not natural.

Take the prophet Samuel, for example. God used him to guide Israel and anoint kings. His mother prayed for a baby, which she promised to dedicate to the Lord. She took Samuel as a child to live in the temple and learn to hear the voice of God and minister unto Him. Every year she made a pilgrimage back to the temple with a suit of clothing for Samuel.

She did that because every year he grew. He started in childhood, but he grew. He grew in faith, in anointing, in discernment.

You are not supposed to stay in the temple and never grow. You are not supposed to go to church and never grow. From time to time you need a larger garment because you are growing. You should grow in vision, in faith, in anointing, and in discernment.

You need to grow in understanding of what God wants for your life. You do not have to stay in childhood; it is time to catch your second "when." God has a bigger garment for you.

God's people are not limited to what happened in the past.

He has something greater for your life than what has happened in the past. Remember, Samuel grew in the temple, and growth requires change.

THE DISTRACTION OF DYSFUNCTION

Don't fall for the python's distraction of dysfunction. So many are held back because they come from a dysfunctional family and feel like God cannot use them. I have news for you—God fixes dysfunction!

Think about Joseph and his family. His daddy's name was Jacob, which means "cheater." He had lied and cheated, and everybody knew it. On top of that, Joseph had brothers who tried to kill him because he wore a different coat. We don't like people who wear different stripes than we wear, especially our brothers. He was thrown into a pit, lied about by Mrs. Potiphar, forgotten by his friends, passed over, and abused.

Joseph had such a relationship with God, though, that he grew in spite of it all. When Potiphar's wife tried to seduce him, Joseph refused her advances. He had God's commands written on his heart. God blessed Joseph as he continued to grow. As an adult Joseph was blessed with a wife and a child.

He named that first child Manasseh, which in Hebrew means, "The Lord has made me to forget." He was not bound to his past. God made him forget it. Instead of giving his son a name that reflected the torment of his past, he named his son for the victory of his future because of his God. Joseph learned it is not what has been done to you, and it is not what you have done, but it is what you *will do* that counts.

Dysfunction was an element in David's family too. David was the "runt of the litter." I like one theory about David's childhood. In Psalm 51:5 David wrote, "Behold, I was brought forth in iniquity, and in sin my mother conceived me." Some Bible commentators believe that David was an illegitimate child. They claim that as the reason David was left out when Samuel told Jesse to bring all his boys for review. Jesse only brought seven out of the eight. According to the theory, Jesse did that because David was not a legitimate son.

Regardless of his past, however, David continued to seek the Lord. He pursued Him, longing to know Him and please Him. As a result, David became stronger as he grew and matured.

Has the enemy been tormenting you with your past? It's not the end of your story! God has a second "when" for you. One key thing to remember is that success is not dependent upon your strength, but it's dependent upon God's. David could have walked away from the battle when he saw the army of Israel pitted against the Philistines.

How many times do we look at situations and think, "Someone else will take care of it"? There are times when God orders your steps and will back you with His strength the moment you are faithful to follow through. David heard the taunts of that giant and said to King Saul:

> "Your servant used to keep his father's sheep, and when a lion or a bear came and took a lamb out of the flock, I went out after it and struck it, and delivered the lamb from its mouth; and when it arose against me, I caught it by its beard, and struck and killed it. Your servant has killed both lion and bear; and this uncircumcised Philistine will be like one of them, seeing he has defied the armies of the living God." Moreover David said, "The LORD, who delivered me from the paw of the lion

and from the paw of the bear, He will deliver me from the hand of this Philistine."

—1 SAMUEL 17:34–37

David was fully aware that God empowered him to protect his flock and rescue the young lamb from the mouth of the predator. He knew it would be no different with that ridiculous giant. The Israelite army was measuring the giant's threats against their own strength and power. David was measuring against his omnipotent God of all creation.

In our weakness, He is always strong. God doesn't need your strength. He wants your weakness and dependency on Him. Goliath was bigger than David; but if the God in you is bigger than the devil in them, it does not matter how big the circumstance. You will win.

There is a new level in God that He wants you to go to. You must be hungry for it and put away childish things. With persistence and faithfulness, build your prayer life, your Bible reading time, your fasting lifestyle, and your worship. When you do, you will move to your second "when."

God doesn't need your strength. He wants your weakness and dependency on Him.

I've often heard the words of Jesus taken out of context when He asked, "When the Son of Man comes, will He really find faith on the earth?" It helps to see that verse in context. In Luke 18:1–8, Jesus was speaking to a group of Pharisees and His disciples.

Then He spoke a parable to them, that men always ought to pray and not lose heart, saying: "There was in a certain city a judge who did not fear God nor regard man. Now there was a widow in that city; and she came to him, saying, 'Get justice for me from my adversary.' And he would not for a while; but afterward he said within himself, 'Though I do not fear God nor regard man, yet because this widow troubles me I will avenge her, lest by her continual coming she weary me.'" Then the Lord said, "Hear what the unjust judge said. And shall God not avenge His own elect who cry out day and night to Him, though He bears long with them? I tell you that He will avenge them speedily. Nevertheless, when the Son of Man comes, will He really find faith on the earth?"

Notice that He began the parable as a lesson that, "Men always ought to pray and not lose heart," and ended it with the question, "When the Son of Man comes, will He really find faith on the earth?" Jesus asks us still today: "When the Son of man comes, will He find the kind of faith that persists in the face of apparent denial and delay?" When everybody else says it's over, that God has left you, will you choose to believe that God is still with you?

When the enemy tries to convince you that it is over for your kids, they will never get their act together—that's not God's voice. Like always, that old serpent is trying to pull you away from God and isolate you so that you will believe his lies.

You need to get that "God is with me" spirit about your future, about your family, about your church, about everything, even your finances. No matter what crisis you may be facing right now, you cannot be victorious with the spirit of the world. Dig deep and find the persistent faith Jesus is seeking.

He is with you—His promise is that you are not alone. He will carry you into your second "when" if you let Him. Do not let python rob from you and limit what God has for you. Instead, rise up in the strength and anointing of the Lord and proclaim, "I don't care what I face today, because God is with me!"

Read on. In the next chapter I'm going to share another tactic of the python—fatal distractions.

ten

FATAL DISTRACTIONS

THE DEVIL TRIED to distract Jesus from His divine purpose, and he will also distract us if we allow it. This is one of the devil's most insidious methods—to deceive, divert, and distract the church from its divine purpose. He parades the most impressive material things in front of us to dazzle and distract us from the ultimate mission God has for our lives.

Sadly, we make this job simple for him because we are easily sidetracked. When we can comfortably continue for months without a fresh sense of the Holy Spirit in our lives, we've been distracted by the devil. When it no longer hurts to have empty altars in our churches, we have been distracted by the devil. When we spend our time and energy debating how best to perpetuate the church rather than how to best reach the world for Jesus Christ, we have been distracted by the devil. When the leaders of our churches become prayerless and are no longer rooted in the Word of God, we have been distracted by the devil.

When these things happen, an invisible, evil force is at work trying to change a spiritual church to a carnal one. The devil distracts the church by quiet displacement and by unnoticed substitution. And before we know it, the spiritual is replaced by the social.

In Acts 16 the python attempted to distract Paul and Silas from their mandate to preach the gospel, and he will do the same to you if you allow him. If you're not careful, the devil's deliberate attempts to keep you from doing the will of God will work.

If we are not prayerful and careful, the enemy will lure us away from the most important things by bringing distractions into our lives—demonic distractions that somehow pull us away from God's true purpose and will for our lives. In my life personally, I believe there are three ways that the python has tried to distract me from the important purpose of God.

EMOTIONAL DISTRACTIONS

The first type of distraction I've watched the enemy use through the years is emotional distractions. An emotional distraction is something that gets you all worked up, but it really doesn't have anything to do with that which is eternal. Let me share an example of when this happened to me.

I remember very clearly a certain politician who years ago was doing things that I believed were diametrically opposed to the Word of God. One particular week I was really upset. I remember that I gathered newspaper clippings and went to my office that Friday, and I shut myself in and I got to work on a sermon. I was going to tell the congregation at Free Chapel how America was going to hell in a handbasket!

But the Lord checked my heart after I thought I was ready to preach, and I discovered a truth in God's Word. When Paul preached, there was a leader by the name of Nero who was persecuting Christians by tarring them and then burning them on poles as lanterns so that he could drive his chariot down the streets of Rome.

They were oppressing the Christians as none of us in the United States have ever experienced. Yet not one time do you ever read that Paul stood up and blasted the government or tried to rally the troops under a political party. But what Paul did do is get up and say, "I preach Christ and Him crucified."

That reminded me that my primary purpose is to deliver people to the foot of the cross. I know that there are social injustices. I know that there is racism. I know that there are terrible abortions that are taking place, and gay marriage, and the list goes on. We should stand firm on what the Scripture says about these things, but I refuse to be brought into huge battles on these and other issues. Because if we're not careful, I believe these things will be used by the enemy to distract the church from its real mission.

Our real mission is not to become a political force in the earth. Our real mission is not to be people who do good things in our society. The real mission of the church—and we must not be distracted from it—is to preach Christ and Him crucified. Paul said in Colossians 1:28, it's Him we preach. We don't preach denominations, we don't preach political parties, and we don't preach my opinion or your opinion. We preach *Him*!

Anything in your life that is pulling you away from intimacy with Jesus is a distraction from the enemy.

We must tell the world that Jesus is the Son of God and that He was born to a virgin by the name of Mary. We must share that He lived a sinless life and that He died on a bloody cross. We must explain that they buried Him in a tomb, but on the third day He rose again, and soon He's coming back. We must never allow the enemy to lure us away from this!

Emotional distractions alienate us from reaching the very people that need the gospel of Jesus Christ. If we're not careful, we just build a society inside of a society called "the church," and we end up reaching no one and accomplishing nothing.

Sometimes people will tell me things like, "I want to quit my job and go into the ministry so I can win souls." Let me help you understand something: all the unsaved people are out there where you work and live! How about saying, "I'm a minister right where I am." Then win somebody for Jesus without being distracted from the purpose of God!

Over the years the enemy has tried to distract me with new methods and new philosophies, but I'm not called to be a counselor. I'm not called to be a doctor who gives you some kind of philosophy that helps you get along in life.

I'm dealing with eternal souls who will face eternal consequences. It's very heavy, and nobody can carry the burden for me. People in other jobs may check out at five and it's over, but my burden never leaves me. I wake up thinking about souls; it's a burden from the Lord. But if I'm not careful, I'll allow the enemy to distract me from what it's all about!

The same is true for you. The enemy will do everything he can to distract you from the Word of God and from prayer. Anything in your life that is pulling you away from intimacy with Jesus is a distraction from the enemy.

OPPORTUNITY DISTRACTIONS

The second distraction is one I call opportunity distractions. A common example of this I've seen over the years is when the Spirit of God moves upon people—let's say it's a young married couple, and an amazingly anointed service touches them. They get up, walk down, clap their hands, weep profusely, and cry out to God. They've been touched and anointed by the Holy Spirit.

The next thing you know, they're involved in everything going on at church—every service, every all-night prayer meeting, every home cell group—they can't get enough! They're on fire, and they start working like you've never seen anybody work. All of this is well and good.

> Too many times the devil dangles a golden carrot out in front of us; he paints some beautiful portrait of prosperity somewhere else and we forget about what God's doing right where we are.

But what happens next is where I see the opportunity distraction come in: a few months later they come to me. "Pastor, we need you to pray. Our heart is torn."

"What's the problem?"

"This church is our life, but the Lord has given us a promotion. We can make three times what we're making. Of course it's going to require us to relocate, we've got to go away, but praise the Lord! Increase is mine!"

Before they can get away, I say, "Have you been there on a weekend and found a church? If God's really in it, there will be a provision spiritually for you."

I'm going to write a really important statement right now: never move for money! I'm going to write it again, since you probably didn't like it the first time: never, never, never, never move for money. Move because God wants you to move. Seek *first* the kingdom, and all these things will follow you!

Not all opportunities are of God. Too many times the devil dangles a golden carrot out in front of us; he paints some beautiful portrait of prosperity somewhere else, and we forget about what God's doing right where we are. There are some things that are more important than a big job and more money. There are some things that are more important than going up the corporate ladder.

It's more important to keep your family together, to keep your children on fire, to keep your own spirit ready for the coming of the Lord Jesus Christ. Sometimes He'll give you what you want, but He'll send you leanness of soul. You'll have money in your pocket, but you'll be empty in your soul. Don't let the devil distract you with opportunity.

Some opportunity distractions don't involve a move. There are folks who will tell me, "Well, Pastor, I don't have to move, and this will increase my pay tremendously and we'll get all the stuff we want. Now, of course, I'll have to give up church because my hours will be on Sundays and Wednesdays. What should I do?"

The answer is simple: if it means *less* God and *more* money, don't do it! Instead, take *more* of God, and you will get everything else you need, because He's *Jehovah Jireh* (the God who provides). The job may go out the door the next week anyhow. David knew what he was talking about when he said, "I would rather be a doorkeeper in the house of my God than dwell in the tents of wickedness" (Ps. 84:10).

Satan offered distractions to Jesus in the wilderness when He was fasting forty days. The devil came to Him and told Him there was an easier way. It didn't take all that prayer business. He didn't have to put Himself through all that.

That's what he's told some of you too. "It doesn't take all of this stuff that you're putting yourself through. Here, I'll give you everything you want. Here's a shortcut; just come bow down to me."

Now what did Jesus say? He said, "It is written, man shall not live by bread alone, but by every word that proceeds out of the mouth of God." In other words, bread and material things are not the sole purpose of my life. The sole purpose of my life is the fresh manna from the ovens of heaven that are in my soul, and if I'm getting *that*, I have something even more important than bread on my table.

> I'm not saying that you shouldn't care about anything or explore new opportunities; I'm saying you don't give your heart to those things.

I'm writing to somebody who's going to read this and wake up out of your slumber! The spirit of Python got in that girl in Acts 16 to distract Paul from what was eternal and what was important. And the enemy will operate like a python to slither into situations and opportunities in your life to sidetrack you.

Do you know how many times people have come to me and said, "Here's a business deal, and you just have to get involved in it. Sign here, here, here, and here." And if I had, I would have lost my ministry and my anointing. At some point you have to choose. The Bible says, "No man that warreth entangleth himself with the affairs of this life" (2 Tim. 2:4, kjv).

We all need jobs, and as I've written at other times in this book, I believe God wants to increase us and enlarge our territories. So I'm not saying that you shouldn't care about anything or explore new opportunities; I'm saying you don't give your heart to those things. Your heart is focused on the call and the purpose of God for your life.

PEOPLE DISTRACTIONS

This third and final distraction is the biggest one! Python really is out to get your victory with this one. You must not allow people to distract you from what God has told and called you to do.

It starts with whom you trust. The Bible talks about three men in 3 John: Gaius, who was generous in hospitality; Demetrius, who was full of good works and of a good reputation; and Diotrephes, who loved "preeminence among them [the brethren]" (v. 9).

To understand what the Bible means when it says he loved "preeminence among them," let me put it in a modern-day setting. I believe Diotrephes had a hefty tithe check, and he used it to try to influence and manipulate the leadership of the church.

Some of the biggest mistakes I've made in my life have been choosing to trust the wrong people. Instead of discerning in the Spirit, I was distracted by people who told me they were with me and were sent by God to help me. I was distracted by their big cars and words of praise. "You're the best thing since cherry pie! You're the most anointed thing I've ever seen in my life. Oh, let me tell you how God has sent me to help you, Pastor."

I'm writing this especially to young pastors and young ministry leaders to try to save you heartache. When people shower you with praise and want to be your new best friend, proceed with caution. They may be a distraction of the enemy. You may find out the hard way that they don't have the spirit of a servant; they want the preeminence. They want to be noticed.

LEARN FROM THE GIBEONITES

In Joshua 9 the Bible says that after Joshua defeated Ai, when the other leaders in the area heard how powerful he was, they brought "bags of vittles." In other words, they brought little bags of goods, or little sacks of money. And they said, "We want to be your servants. We want to be your friends."

The elders of Israel did not consult the Lord before making a league with these other leaders, the Gibeonites. Be careful, my friend. Don't fall for it just because they look good, just because they sound good. You better consult with the Lord.

"Well, I'm going to marry him," you say. Did you consult with the Lord? If not, you might wake up one day and realize you're married to someone who doesn't care anything at all about the cost of following Jesus. He just wants to have a "normal" life.

Now do you see how dangerous it can be when the python distracts you with the wrong people?

The devil will bring people into your life who look like the right people, sound like the right people, and act like the right people, but they are the *wrong* people. Be careful! The wrong people will mess you up!

Aside from the wrong people who can derail you, there are any number of ways that even the right people in your life can cause distractions that can steal your attention: interruptions, crises, disagreements, phone calls, e-mails, text messages, Twitter, Facebook—in fact, social media is one giant people distraction!

The devil will bring people into your life who look like the right people, sound like the right people, and act like the right people, but they are the *wrong* people. Be careful!

Watch out. When I get bombarded with people distractions, I've found it's often right when we're about to break into a mighty revival. Or it will happen right after a great move of the Spirit. Sometimes I can almost sit and count the seconds until it happens: a powerful move of God on Sunday, and...wait for it...wait for it...somebody's mad by Monday.

CAST IT OUT

If you've had enough of people distractions, opportunity distractions, and emotional distractions, you have to make up your mind, like Paul, that you're going to cast that devil out. You have to understand the spiritual activity, the agenda of the python, to get you off course from God's purpose in your life.

As I write this, I know I'm writing to someone who really needs to hear this message: Be careful, because there are distracting spirits that have come to pull you off course from what God has really called you to do. People, opportunities, and even emotional ties to things will get you off course. If this is happening to you, lift up your hands and say, "Lord, I surrender to Your will."

The Lord spoke to me about all this through the Gibeonites in Joshua 9. When the Israelites made a league with these Gibeonites and let them travel and become a part of them, the Gibeonites continually had to be managed and defended. If Gibeon ever got in a fight with somebody, Israel had to come fight for them.

Israel had to spend time and resources managing and defending these "friends" for the rest of their existence. And that's what happens to us. We let the wrong people in. We take the job that keeps us away from the house of God. We jump on the latest political bandwagon. Then we have to spend our time and resources to manage it, and we have to defend why it's there all the time. We don't have time to be about our Father's business. We don't have time to focus on the things that matter for eternity.

Whom am I writing to? Who has compromised? Who has been distracted? I'm not talking about whether you go to church all the time; I'm talking about your heart condition. Guard your heart, Scripture says (Prov. 4:23). The deceitfulness of riches and the cares of this life choke out fruitfulness (Matt. 13:22).

I'm going to tell you what means more to God than big buildings, fancy churches, and plush campuses. He is looking for hearts that will break before Him and make vows of commitment to not be distracted from eternity. That's what pleases the Lord; that's the church Jesus is coming back for. I have news for you; He isn't coming back for some old bride that's had her teeth knocked out by the devil, wearing an old, dirty dress.

He's coming back for a glorious bride who is radiant with love for Him. When she walks in the back door, the whole world is going to look in amazement at her glory, at her purity! She walks down that aisle and turns around, I see in my spirit, she's going to pull her dress up just a little, and she's going to be wearing combat boots!

I'm going to tell you what means more to God than big buildings, fancy churches, and plush campuses. He is looking for hearts that will break before Him and make vows of commitment to not be distracted from eternity.

It's time to go to war against the powers of darkness that want to steal, kill, and destroy. It's time to put on your combat boots and kick the python out of your life. In the next section I will help you understand several very important ways that you can defeat him. You don't have to be his prey any longer. Read on!

NO LONGER
HIS PREY!

eleven

THE POWER OF PRAYER

NOTICE THAT THE spirit of Python came against Paul and Silas in Acts 16:16 as they went to prayer—and BOOM! Python showed up. The python tactics of the enemy come to squeeze prayer out of your life. The ability to detect this is critical. It's not just natural things that keep you from prayer. The devil knows your greatest weapon against his kingdom is your voice, your prayer life. Prayer will usher you into the presence, power, and purpose of God.

My mother comes from a very large family. When she was fourteen years old, her mother died from a heart attack at the young age of thirty-eight. She had just had a child five days before. She was the mother of eighteen children. My mom at the age of fourteen began to take care of all those children in eastern North Carolina.

She had developed at a young age a powerful prayer life. She would pray in the family garden; she set up an old-fashioned altar with a bench where she could go into that garden and have private times of prayer.

One day when she was twenty years old, she was praying in that garden and had a vision of a young man with black, wavy hair driving a green car. A few days later the man who would be my dad showed up at her doorstep. He was an evangelist preaching at a revival in the area, and he had met her before and decided to come to the house.

She told me how she was cleaning the tile in the bathrooms and went to the door. She was stunned to see a man standing there with black wavy hair and his green Buick in the driveway. He asked her to come to the revival where he was preaching. She and one of her brothers went to the revival, and so began their courtship to marriage.

She said that after praying and seeing the vision of the young man with the black hair and green car, she knew God was telling her that someone was coming into her life soon. She found the purpose, plan, and will of God for her life in that garden (her prayer place). You can still find God's perfect will when you pray.

The most powerful people on the face of this earth are those who have learned how to pray. Not people who merely believe in prayer, or talk about prayer, or those who can teach beautiful lessons on how to pray—but people who *take time to pray*.

That means they take time away from other things, important things, pressing and urgent things. We all have such "things" in our lives. Those who prevail are the ones who take that time to pray *first* and then schedule all the other "things" afterward. They understand that "prayer first" is the key to victory.

Prayer changes the atmosphere and shifts things in the spirit realm. In Paul's letter to the Thessalonian church he exhorted them to "pray without ceasing" (1 Thess. 5:17). Prayer is that holy communication with heaven that creates an atmosphere for God's presence, but the devil's python strategy is to stop or hinder your prayer life. When it is time to pray, if you watch TV instead, python is hindering you.

The devil knows the greatest weapon we have is not

evangelists or pastors; our greatest weapon is prayer. When we begin to pray, hell's foundations are shaken. When we begin to pray, there is a Holy Ghost outpouring. When we begin to pray, earthquakes will happen in the Spirit. The enemy is not afraid of how long we shout. He is afraid of how deeply we pray.

If a man can pray, he can do anything. Heaven and earth will take notice, because prayer is the power on earth that moves the power in heaven. Prayer is God saying, "If you will, I will. If you will pray, I will act. If you will pray, I will move. If you will ask, I will answer. I will release My best into your life."

PREVAILING PRAYER

The holy men and women of God who subdue hell's threats are praying men and women. Prevailing prayer is vital in the life of every believer.

The enemy is not afraid of how long we shout.
He is afraid of how deeply we pray.

What is "prevailing" prayer? First let me tell you what it is not. It is not personal charisma. It is not programs. It is not education. Prayer is not advertising, marketing, architectural design, or beautiful facilities. Without prayer, all of those things mean nothing.

Prevailing prayer is not "foxhole praying," when you only pray when you get in trouble. Prevailing prayer is that consistent, insistent, continual life of communication with God. It's not something you *do*; it is a part of who you *are*. It is a part of what Christ means to you. You cannot separate it from who you are. With that kind of life of prayer you will know victory. Everything God wants to do is linked to prayer.

A good example of prevailing prayer is Moses standing in the gap before God on behalf of the Israelites. While Moses was meeting with God on Mt. Sinai, receiving the Ten Commandments, the people of Israel were building a golden calf-idol and corrupting themselves with drink and debauchery.

> And the LORD said to Moses, "I have seen this people, and indeed it is a stiff-necked people! Now therefore, let Me alone, that My wrath may burn hot against them and I may consume them. And I will make of you a great nation."
>
> —EXODUS 32:9–10

God was going to give Moses a promotion, but as for the rest, He was about to wipe the slate clean and start over. After spending time with God, Moses's great concern was for God's name and honor among the heathen nations. He was worried about what they would say about a God that wiped out His own people. So Moses interposed himself between the sinful people and the judgment of God, pleading:

> Turn from your fierce anger; relent and do not bring disaster on your people. Remember your servants Abraham, Isaac and Israel, to whom you swore by your own self: "I will make your descendants as numerous as the stars in the sky and I will give your descendants all this land I promised them, and it will be their inheritance forever."
>
> —EXODUS 32:12–13, NIV

Moses's prevailing prayer caused the Lord to relent from destroying all the people. What is prevailing prayer? It is Joshua in battle, coming to the aid of Gibeon. The Lord promised him victory over the enemy, but the day was slipping away. So Joshua prayed, "Sun, stand still over Gibeon; and Moon, in the Valley of Aijalon" (Josh. 10:12). His prayer stopped time until the battle was over.

Prevailing prayer is Hezekiah after he received the threatening letter from Sennacherib, king of Assyria, boasting that God would not protect him or Jerusalem from destruction (Isa. 37). Instead of internalizing that fear, Hezekiah went in faith and presented the letter to the Lord. "Then the angel of the LORD went out, and killed in the camp of the Assyrians one hundred and eighty-five thousand; and when people arose early in the morning, there were the corpses—all dead" (v. 36).

In Isaiah 38 Hezekiah was faced with a death sentence. He cried out to God, who heard his prayer and granted him fifteen more years. I believe prevailing prayer can win battles, it can add years to your life, it can conquer cancer, it can defeat heart disease, and it can cause a stroke to turn around and go back where it came from.

Prevailing prayer was necessary to cast a demon out of a young boy. Jesus was returning with Peter, James, and John from the mountain where they witnessed the supernatural transfiguration. As they approached, a desperate father made his way through the crowd. He had a son who had been afflicted by a demon of epilepsy since his birth. He had taken the boy to the other disciples, but they were not able to help. So he knelt down before Jesus and pleaded with Him to help. "Jesus rebuked the demon, and it came out of him; and the child was cured from that very hour" (Matt. 17:18).

Later the disciples wanted to know why they had not been able to cast it out. Jesus answered, "Because of your unbelief; for assuredly, I say to you, if you have faith as a mustard seed, you will say to this mountain, 'Move from here to there,' and it will move; and nothing will be impossible for you. However, this kind does not go out except by prayer and fasting" (vv. 20–21).

Prevailing prayer breaks the faith barrier.

The other nine disciples had enjoyed Jesus's presence but had not learned to assimilate His power in their lives. A lot of times we get into God's presence, but it doesn't do anything for us in real life. We don't learn to draw from His presence and use that to operate in His power and authority. The man in Matthew 17 brought his son to the disciples with a plea of "help me." They tried, but they could not help. They were lacking time in prayer, time in fasting—and faith.

> Even though you cannot be everywhere your children are all the time, your prayers can be. You can bind and loose and take authority.

Once when Jesus was returning from a time of private prayer, a disciple asked, "Lord, teach us to pray, as John also taught his disciples" (Luke 11:1).

That request came from the heart of a man who had seen something precious. I wonder if he followed Jesus to His secret prayer place and hid at a distance while the Lord prayed. He watched and listened, as the Son talked to the Father. What an unforgettable moment as heaven's glory surrounded the Lord of lords. No wonder he wanted to be taught how to pray the same way—the way a son talks to a father.

Keep in mind that, up to this point, the disciples essentially stayed with the Lord because they believed an earthly kingdom was coming. Accounts indicate some of them were even jockeying for a position of authority in the new kingdom.

So He said to them, "When you pray, say: Our Father in heaven, hallowed be Your name. Your kingdom come. Your will be done on earth as it is in heaven. Give us day by day our daily bread. And forgive us our sins, for we also forgive everyone who is indebted to us. And do not lead us into temptation, but deliver us from the evil one."

—LUKE 11:2–4

He went on to tell them the parable of the man knocking at his friend's door at midnight to borrow some bread. Jesus told them, "I say to you, though he will not rise and give to him because he is his friend, yet because of his persistence he will rise and give him as many as he needs" (v. 8). From this He explained:

Ask, and it will be given to you; seek, and you will find; knock, and it will be opened to you. For everyone who asks receives, and he who seeks finds, and to him who knocks it will be opened. If a son asks for bread from any father among you, will he give him a stone? Or if he asks for a fish, will he give him a serpent instead of a fish? Or if he asks for an egg, will he offer him a scorpion? If you then, being evil, know how to give good gifts to your children, how much more will your heavenly Father give the Holy Spirit to those who ask Him!

—LUKE 11:9–13

Matthew also recorded the Lord teaching them:

> Whatever you bind on earth will be bound in heaven, and whatever you loose on earth will be loosed in heaven.
>
> —MATTHEW 18:18

That first-century New Testament church walked in amazing power! Sadly that is the opposite of what we often see in today's church. Jesus taught the disciples that there is no distance in prayer, and there are no barriers on prayer. When we pray, we project ourselves—and His kingdom—into the situation.

Even though you cannot be everywhere your children are all the time, your prayers can be. You can bind and loose and take authority. You cannot be in the White House, but your prayers can get there and impose the will of God into the atmosphere.

Sometimes it takes persistence before you see results. You are in the midst of a struggle, and you pray and pray, yet it seems nothing changes. It has happened to me before. But you decide to push harder and pray once more. Suddenly it is as if heaven breaks open and the victory is won.

We need to shake off the coils of python and stir up the power of prayer in our lives! Are you concerned about a friend whose marriage is marked by violence? Prayer can get in where you cannot. Are there bad influences in your children's lives? Are there things coming against your marriage, your home, or your finances? Prayer goes to the middle of the situation and puts the python in a headlock!

Jesus taught two important things about prayer: *pattern* and *persistence*.

PATTERN

The Bible says that Jesus only did what His Father told Him to do. How did Jesus know what God wanted? He made a habit of praying (Luke 5:16). We think we can make huge decisions based on experience and wisdom alone. We think we can choose a spouse based on butterflies and emotions alone. Yet the Son of God did nothing on His own without prayer. One hour in the presence of God will reveal any flaws in your most carefully laid plans.

> The only limit to prayer is how limited it is in our lives.

After Jesus miraculously multiplied the bread and fish to feed five thousand people, He sent the disciples by boat across the Sea of Galilee to Gennesaret. Then, "He went up on the mountain by Himself to pray" (Matt. 14:23).

You can't walk on water, calm storms, and heal the masses publicly without first dealing with them in the secret place of prayer. When I read verses like, "Now in the morning, having risen a long while before daylight, He went out and departed to a solitary place; and there He prayed" (Mark 1:35), I like to say that Jesus was "putting a deposit down" so that He could "write spiritual checks" all day long.

Too many Christians write spiritual checks without making a prayer deposit, so they bounce all over the place. If you want to write spiritual checks all day, get up and pray before you go out of the house. Then you can speak to the mountain, and it will move. Then you can say, "Today I'll have good success, and I'll heal the sick, and I can represent Christ." It all depends on making that deposit, fighting the battles in prayer *first*. The only limit to prayer is how limited it is in our lives.

We have storms that are unsubdued. We have multitudes who are unhealed. We have angels who are unemployed. Our choices often backfire because we are writing checks on empty accounts.

I've had people tell me, "I don't understand, Pastor. I prayed and nothing happened." The truth is, they commanded and spoke to the storm in the middle of the storm without making a deposit before the storm came.

You see victory when you live your life storing up prevailing prayer. Then, when you stand in the storm, you know who you are and what authority you have.

PERSISTENCE

In the Old Testament Daniel was a man of authority in prayer. There was war in the heavenlies, and Daniel was persistently praying and fasting for the restoration of Israel. He received an amazing visitation from an angel who told him, "Do not fear, Daniel, for from the first day that you set your heart to understand, and to humble yourself before your God, your words were heard; and I have come because of your words. But the prince of the kingdom of Persia withstood me twenty-one days" (Dan. 10:12–13).

He was telling Daniel that God heard his request the first day, but demonic forces had battled against him. Persistent prayers fuel the fight and bring the breakthrough. When a specific miracle has left the hand of God for you, the devil, like a python, will fight to choke out your prayer life.

Do you understand that the first day he prayed the answer left the hand of God? Too often, if we don't see the answer right away, we give up. I believe there are miracles that have already left the throne room, but they are floating around in the spirit realm somewhere because we are not faithful to pray them in.

However, *faith* says, "I will pray. I will knock. I will ask. I will seek until I get my deliverance." "For everyone who asks receives, and he who seeks finds, and to him who knocks it will be opened" (Matt. 7:8). There is no *sometimes* in that statement.

The only way to learn how to pray is to pray. Open your mouth and start saying things to God. That's how you pray. Say exactly what you're feeling in your heart.

Speak out loud. Prayer is not a quiet thing. That is why python seeks to choke out breath—it takes breath to speak!

I believe there are miracles that have already left the throne room, but they are floating around in the spirit realm somewhere because we are not faithful to pray them in.

Some of the most powerful praying you can do is when you speak back to God what He said to you through His Word. Pray the Word. Don't worry if you think you don't know how to do this. It's easy. Simply open the Bible and start praying the Word back to Him. Find the promises in His Word, and start saying them back to God.

Paul tells us that, "Faith comes by hearing, and hearing by the word of God" (Rom. 10:17). Praying His Word back to Him builds faith, and faith energizes prayer.

Peter addressed the awed crowd after the lame man was healed, saying, "His name, through faith in His name, has made this man strong" (Acts 3:16). Without faith, prayer does not do you any good. You can repeat faithless prayers until you are blue in the face, but it is the prayer of faith that changes things.

Faith gives your prayers the power to produce in your life. So, if you're asking for something and don't really believe it's going to happen, quit praying. You're wasting time. We need to enter into the faith dimension that energizes prayer. Read on to discover how to break through the limiting python spirit with faith.

twelve

THE POWER OF FAITH

ANY YEARS AGO we were in a building program at the church. We were building a youth and media center, and the cost was over $3 million. We had saved over $900,000 and had secured a loan from a local bank for the remainder of the money to complete the project. The church was exploding with growth, and the ministry was becoming more prominent in our community and surrounding areas.

I guess you could say we were "the talk of the town." Denominational and racial barriers were being torn down for the first time in our small, Southern community. In short, God was "pouring out His Spirit upon all flesh," and our congregation represented that outpouring. We were growing by the hundreds.

There were some in our community who were not fans of our church and didn't like the fact that a "Spirit-filled church" was growing. I believe spiritually we began to attract the attention of the spirit of the enemy. In praying and fasting for revival, we were seeing many saved and filled with the Holy Spirit. During this time period we even broke out into a five-week revival with evangelist Perry Stone.

As we began our building program, we used the cash reserves we had saved and then went to make the first withdrawal on our secured loan. To our great surprise, the bank and its board of directors refused to give us the money with no explanation. I asked for a meeting with the president of the bank. At that meeting I was told that they had changed their minds and were no longer interested in being part of our church's growth.

I was perplexed and shocked. We had impeccable credit. We were a blessing to our community through many outreaches. What would we do? The building project was in full swing, the steel beams were up, but we suddenly had no more money to draw upon.

Looking back, I believe with all my heart that this was an attack from our unseen enemy to restrict and coil around our church to stop us from reaching thousands of souls. I told the bank president in our meeting that if they didn't keep their word and give us the money as promised for the loan, I would inform our congregation of their actions. He grinned and smugly said, "Do what you like, but we will not change our minds."

That Sunday morning I got up and shared my heavy heart with our congregation. It felt like our vision to reach our city, state, and nation was stopped in its tracks. Our media department, our offices, and many outreach ministries were to be in that building as well.

I shared with the congregation the bad news, and then I challenged them to do what I was going to do. I had made up my mind to remove my personal bank account from that bank.

That evening an elderly, trusted minister named E. L. Terry came to our church and shared that God had told him that what had happened with the bank would turn out for our good. He said that we would not need the loan because God was going to bless Free Chapel so that we could build the new building and be debt free. The church exploded into thunderous claps.

The next morning the parking lot of the bank was full. There were nine or ten customers in each line. They were saying, "I'm from Free Chapel and will be closing my account."

By noon that day I received a call asking me to attend an emergency meeting the bank had called with its board. When I arrived, they presented a contract for the loan and said "Preacher, you have just about ruined our bank." I was told that more than five million dollars had been withdrawn from the bank that day. I then informed the president of the bank along with the board members in attendance that we would no longer need the loan and that we were going to trust God.

> You may hit barriers in your faith walk, but do not let that discourage you. Barriers can be broken. You can go as high as you believe God can take you.

I can't explain to you exactly what happened over the next few months. All I know is that every week we would tell the church how much we needed financially, and every week for almost a year we met that need miraculously. Some weeks we needed $350,000 or more above our operating expenses to pay the bills. Every week God supplied the need.

The python's grip on our finances and our faith had been broken. We moved into our new building debt free for the glory of God. When you begin to praise, you begin to pray; when you begin to fast and to give, your faith is increased. And the power of your faith breaks the power of python off of your finances and off of your dreams.

The python spirit wants to limit your growth and limit

your finances, but he will not succeed because, "Greater is He who is in you than he who is in the world" (1 John 4:4, NAS). By faith, as you read this chapter, I speak expansion, growth, increase, and the financial resources you need to fulfill God's call upon your life. May you have the faith to do what God has called you to do.

LEVELS OF FAITH

There are levels of faith that we grow and walk in. Paul talked about how "the righteousness of God is revealed from faith to faith; as it is written, 'The just shall live by faith'" (Rom. 1:17). There are multilevels of faith, and faith grows as you grow in God.

In 2 Thessalonians 1:3 Paul said of the people of that church, "Your faith grows exceedingly, and the love of every one of you all abounds toward each other." Faith is one of the fruit of the Spirit. Fruit isn't just produced at full maturity. It starts out as a seed, grows into a tree, produces a bloom that fades to reveal the immature fruit, and then the fruit is nurtured until it reaches maturity. Our faith in God has to be constantly fed, nurtured, and cultivated.

You may hit barriers in your faith walk, but do not let that discourage you. Barriers can be broken. You can go as high as you believe God can take you.

What is the highest level of faith? I believe that answer can be found in Galatians 5:6, "The only thing that counts is faith expressing itself through love" (NIV). Faith works by love. The highest level of faith is *perfect love.*

Perfect love is love without an agenda. Perfect love forgives. When you move into the realm of perfect love, you enter into what Jesus entered into when He went to the cross. The last thing Jesus said before He died on the cross was, "Father, forgive them." That is the highest level of faith. The number one thing that makes your faith work is not just your confession—and I believe in confession. The highest level of faith is love.

We don't have to wrestle with the gates of hell. We need to break the prayer barrier and move in faith into perfect love. We have the keys to the gates, but we must break through to the highest level of faith to use them.

If those keys will work on the gates of hell, they will work anywhere—the keys to financial blessings, the keys to miracles and healing, the keys to signs and wonders in the church. When the church moves in love, miracles start happening.

Are we really trying to accommodate what God wants to do in these last days? We read about revival overseas, but are we ready to go to a level of perfect love where we can see it in the church in America?

More Than Positive Thinking

Remember, in the scheme of python, the plan is to steal your breath and silence your voice. One time when I was praying, I sensed the Lord telling me, "I do not need another motivational preacher." I really had to stop and think about that for a while.

> I can't "coach" the python out of your life. It takes more than positive thinking or motivational speeches to break free from his deadly grip.

There is a place in the body of Christ for those who encourage, motivate, and coach others; there is nothing wrong with that. But I'm not a life coach. I'm not a motivational speaker. I'm called to preach fiery, Spirit-filled messages and pray fiery, Spirit-filled prayers. I'm called to raise up a remnant of sold-out Christians who live life in light of eternity.

We have been given spiritual weapons in this battle that go beyond "positive thinking." Paul made it clear that these weapons are "mighty in God for pulling down strongholds, casting down arguments and every high thing that exalts itself against the knowledge of God, bringing every thought into captivity to the obedience of Christ, and being ready to punish all disobedience when your obedience is fulfilled" (2 Cor. 10:4–6).

I can't "coach" the python out of your life. It takes more than positive thinking or motivational speeches to break free from his deadly grip. It takes spiritual warfare. You have to have zero tolerance for sin, distractions, or any other thing in your life that gives an open door to the python and his demons. You must take a bold stand against the weapons of darkness through the authority of Christ and open your mouth in prayer and praise to your God.

When you are not living an obedient, prayerful life, your level of consecration is lowered, more and more sin is tolerated rather than overcome, and your standards of righteousness are torn down by the heavy influence of the world. When you are not praying, you are inviting that spirit of the world to come in like a python and suffocate the breath of God out of you. Isaiah 59:19 promised, "When the enemy comes in like a flood, the Spirit of the LORD will lift up a standard against him." Are you leaving the floodgates open through prayerlessness?

You need to pray and seek holiness until sin becomes exceedingly sinful to you again. You must grow in faith. Growth comes from love. Writing to the church in Ephesus, Paul said, "That we should no longer be children, tossed to and fro and carried about with every wind of doctrine, by the trickery of men, in the cunning craftiness of deceitful plotting, but, speaking the truth in love, may grow up in all things into Him who is the head—Christ" (Eph. 4:14–15).

If you are going to walk in faith, break the barrier, and move into a new dimension, it will be because you take risks, because you determine not to become satisfied, because you make a conscious decision to push on to greater things. I believe God is looking for people who will dare to break out of comfortable places and say, "I'm going to another level."

Break through the barriers and limitations of the enemy. Go to another level, and expect God to do something in your life that is so powerful that you will know nothing is impossible through faith in His name.

> Faith reaches up and grabs nothing until it becomes something. Faith grabs hold of a promise in the heavenlies and will not let go until you see it manifested in your life.

Elijah was a man who broke the faith barrier. He boldly proclaimed to the wicked, idolatrous leadership of Israel that there would be no rain in the land, the rain would cease and begin at his word (1 Kings 17:1).

Finally, after three years of drought, the Word of God came to Elijah. He told Ahab to go eat and drink because he could hear "the sound of abundance of rain" (1 Kings 18:41). Then Elijah went up to the top of Mt. Carmel, bowed down, and told his servant to go and look toward the sea. His servant looked but saw nothing. Seven times Elijah sent him back to look again. Seven times the servant obeyed.

Finally, the last time, he came back and reported with excitement, "There is a cloud, as small as a man's hand, rising out of the sea!" (v. 44). The clouds rolled in and the rain came down, just as Elijah said.

Persistence will break the faith barrier. Faith reaches up and grabs nothing until it becomes something. Faith grabs hold of a promise in the heavenlies and will not let go until you see it manifested in your life. Elijah went from just knowing God's Word to moving in the reality of it by faith.

Paul said that his preaching was not "persuasive words of human wisdom," but a demonstration of the Spirit's power (1 Cor. 2:4). It is one thing to know the Word, proclaim the Word, and preach the Word. It is one thing to talk about healing, talk about miracles, talk about salvation, or talk about household blessing, but I want to *see these things take place!* It is time for a faith breakthrough. We need to share the gospel *and* demonstrate it as well.

GET READY FOR NEW LEVELS

The prophet Ezekiel had an interesting encounter with an angel of the Lord. He wrote, "Then he brought me back to the door of the temple; and there was water, flowing from under the threshold of the temple toward the east" (Ezek. 47:1).

Most people focus on the river flowing from the temple when they read this passage, but I want you to notice that Scripture says the angel of the Lord brought him *back* to that door. That means he had been at the door before.

I wonder how many times we get to the point where all we need to do is just press through the door and we will go to a new level, but instead we become fearful, or we become too comfortable, and we back up. And God has to keep bringing us to the door over and over and over again.

Remember, He will bring you to it, but He will not push you through it. Only your faith will break the barrier to the next level. Just on the other side there is an exciting new season that is about to break loose in your life. You can't give up, and you can't back up.

The python is going to "put the squeeze on" right when you are on the brink of a breakthrough. But once you pass that brink, you enter a realm in the Spirit that you just can't get over. It messes you up for life. You move into it, and you cannot do anything but flow with what God is doing—completely flowing with the river of God, just like Ezekiel's vision in Ezekiel 47.

It is one thing to talk about healing, talk about miracles, talk about salvation, or talk about household blessing, but I want to see these things take place!

God wants you to break some faith barriers and go deeper. Don't let the entanglements of the world hold you back. Get to the place where you tap into something you can't get over; it radically changes your life, and you're flowing with it because you can't control it.

Persistence breaks the faith barrier. The church needs to change from being an audience to an army. We need to be "gone with the wind." Jesus said, "The wind blows where it wishes, and you hear the sound of it, but cannot tell where it comes from and where it goes. So is everyone who is born of the Spirit" (John 3:8).

The Holy Spirit of God goes in whatever direction He wants to go, and He invites you along for the amazing ride of faith.

Whatever God wants to do, you should be willing to yield and bend to His perfect will. I promise you, if you seriously go with God, you will not stay where you are, nor will you go back to the past.

God wants you to break through. He wants you to move into a new dimension, into the highest level of faith. Use your faith. Go to a new level. Enter into the perfect love realm where faith works.

He Wants to Do Something Greater

The goal of the python is to put limitation on you, but God is the God of maximum capacity. Whatever you are believing Him for, believe Him for the maximum and enlarge your capacity. In chapter 9 I explained the limiting mind-set the enemy tries to get you to believe. Get past what you think is "big" and catch a vision for what God really wants to do in your life.

> The church needs to change from being an audience to an army.

As Paul proclaimed, "Now to Him who is able to do exceedingly abundantly above all that we ask or think, according to the power that works in us, to Him be glory in the church by Christ Jesus to all generations, forever and ever" (Eph. 3:20–21). He wants to do much bigger than you are asking and believing Him for right now.

There is no way for you to know what you are fully capable of doing when you trust God. It is believed that the great evangelist D. L. Moody said the following words to his sons just before he died: "If God be your partner, make your plans large."

When you give God more and more of yourself, He enlarges your capacity.

If you offer God five minutes, He will fill it. If you offer God an hour, He will fill it. If you offer God twenty-one days of fasting and prayer, He will fill it. If you offer God your whole life, He will fill it. He is a God of capacity.

You have to enlarge your capacity. Do not let the enemy restrict or limit you. God wants you to believe Him for bigger things. Pray and believe for what God knows you are capable of. This can be your season to break through the biggest barriers you have ever faced. Every life has options and choices. When God speaks His Word over your life, you can believe what you hear and be confident that it will change your reality.

When you encounter your purpose, you will step into something that God has known about you and planned for you the whole time. It doesn't matter what else someone has called you in life. What Jesus says is all that matters.

God has already spoken your destiny over you. That is why the enemy tries so hard to steer you away, distract you, or squeeze the life out of you. He never wants you to get to the place where God can fill you to capacity. You will never reach your full purpose as long as you remain small on the inside. You increase your capacity through journeys of faith and trusting Him.

God wants you to have heaven's view of who you really are. We think too small. We dream too tiny. We expect too little. But there is a divine destiny to your life.

I remember when it happened for me. As a teenager going into my twentieth birthday, God called me to preach. The heavens were opened unto me, and I saw myself preaching. I saw myself going all over the world sharing the gospel.

God loves to be believed! God wants you to know that if you just believe Him, all things are possible. He can enlarge your capacity.

"'For I know the plans I have for you,' declares the Lord, 'plans to prosper you and not to harm you, plans to give you hope and a future'" (Jer. 29:11, NIV). Those are God's plans for you. Break free from the python's limiting grasp through a prayer of faith and perfect love. Believe God for more in your life.

> It doesn't matter what else someone has called you in life. What Jesus says is all that matters.

In the next chapter we'll add the next step—the power of praise—as a powerful weapon to keep us from becoming the prey of the python.

thirteen

THE POWER OF PRAISE

WHAT KEEPS YOU awake at night? Do you ever experience anxiety that prevents you from sleeping? Thoughts about unpaid bills, job cuts, family strife, protecting your kids, and much more can rob you of the rest that God promises. Solomon said, "It is vain for you to rise up early, to sit up late, to eat the bread of sorrows; for so He gives His beloved sleep" (Ps. 127:2).

I don't appreciate the devil trying to keep me up at night. In fact, it is time that the children of God start giving the devil nightmares; robbing him of sleep rather than the other way around. It isn't that hard to do—all it takes is some serious praise.

I love the story of Gideon and how God mightily used that ordinary guy from the smallest tribe of Israel to defeat an oppressive army. Israel had sinned and had begun to worship the demon gods of the Amorites. Things grew increasingly worse until God finally turned them over to their enemy, the Midianites. The oppression was so bad the people fled to the mountains and caves. Even there the Midianites and others ravaged the land, destroying the crops and herds. They impoverished Israel, and the people began to cry out to God for help.

Gideon was hidden in the winepress, threshing wheat, in an attempt to protect what little harvest his family managed to keep from the enemy. God sent an angel to talk to Gideon and remind him that he was a mighty man of valor. Of course, hiding in the winepress after being beaten down by the enemy for so many years, Gideon did not feel mighty or valiant.

It's a good thing God sees more in us than we see in ourselves. We need to keep the python's limiting lies far from our minds if we want to see ourselves the way God does.

The Lord will call you to get past what you think is "big" so you can walk into the destiny He has planned for you. God said to Gideon, "Go in the strength you have and save Israel out of Midian's hand. Am I not sending you?" (Judg. 6:14, NIV).

Citing his many shortcomings, Gideon asked how he—one man—could possibly defeat a vast, cruel army that had brutally oppressed all of Israel for so long. God replied, "I will be with you, and you will strike down all the Midianites together" (v. 16, NIV).

In other words, God had already given Gideon the victory. All Gideon had to do was walk out and express that victory. Praise is an expression of victory.

As God's people we need to understand that we have been positioned for victory through the death and the resurrection of Jesus Christ. We have been positioned to turn hell into pandemonium. We are not, as the end-time church, supposed to stay in a defensive mode, beaten up by the enemy as we try to barely make it through the trials of life. Enough of the "demon"-strations; it is time for a clear *demonstration* of God's anointing in the life of the believer that shakes the gates of hell off their hinges.

God says, "I will be with you." God is your refuge. God is your strength. God and God alone is your victory!

The Midianite army was camped out for the night in the

valley. To build Gideon's confidence, the Lord told him to go down to the enemy's camp and listen to what was being said. So Gideon took a buddy down the hill with him. They carefully made their way to one of the tents.

> Enough of the "demon"-strations; it is time for a clear *demonstration* of God's anointing in the life of the believer that shakes the gates of hell off their hinges.

Why would God tell Gideon to go listen in the middle of the night when the enemy should have been sound asleep? Simple: the tables had turned, and it was time for the enemy to have nightmares. One soldier woke up his tent mate to tell him about the dream he had.

> "A round loaf of barley bread came tumbling into the Midianite camp. It struck the tent with such force that the tent overturned and collapsed." His friend responded, "This can be nothing other than the sword of Gideon son of Joash, the Israelite. God has given the Midianites and the whole camp into his hands."
> —Judges 7:13–14, niv

We should not be the ones tossing and turning all night. We should not be filled with fear and anxiety. When the people of God are worried, the wrong camp is worried. We need to cause a nightmare in the camp of the enemy.

Gideon returned to his small band of three hundred soldiers. He gave each one a trumpet, an empty pitcher, and a torch to hide under the pitcher. They divided into three groups and surrounded the camp of the enemy on three sides.

"Then the three companies blew the trumpets and broke

the pitchers—they held the torches in their left hands and the trumpets in their right hands for blowing—and they cried, 'The sword of the LORD and of Gideon!'" (Judg. 7:20). It caused such fear and confusion in the enemy's camp that they turned on each other, killing one another as they fled.

PRAISE CREATES NIGHTMARES FOR THE ENEMY

We are equipped to cause nightmares for the enemy. One of the greatest threats to the enemy is a broken vessel. One of the three "weapons" of Gideon's army was broken clay pitchers. But God used those broken vessels to defeat the enemy. It is not your strength but your brokenness that God uses. It is not your gift but your yieldedness; it is not your independence but your dependence on Him that prevails.

Do you know what the devil wants you to do? He wants you to just lie down and let him plow over you. He wants you to give him no resistance. Isaiah 51:23 says, "Lie down, that we may walk over you."

God's people have bowed down to the enemy far too long. He has run over the church long enough. He has run over God's people long enough. He has run over your life long enough. He has wrapped himself around you and choked you long enough. Give up, let down your guard, and he will overtake you—or *resist*, and he will flee.

Resist sickness. Resist depression. Resist fear. Resist divorce. Resist poverty. Resist lack and limitation. Stand up and say, "No! I'm not bowing down for you to run me over. I'm not going to give you a foothold so that you can gain higher ground. I resist you in the name of the Lord!"

Paul and Silas were arrested and revival broke out. They were beaten and thrown into prison. But at midnight the two began to pray and praise God. If they couldn't sleep, neither would the devil. Paul started singing. Silas joined in and made it a duet. God made it a trio, and that old jailhouse started to tremble.

You can bring God into your circumstances—out of brokenness, out of darkness, out of a beating—when you begin to praise Him. Revival broke out, and prison doors opened. If your problems are keeping you up at night, it is time to start keeping the devil up with your praise.

> It is not your strength, but your brokenness that God uses. It is not your gift but your yieldedness; it is not your independence, but your dependence on Him that prevails.

We need to see who we are in Christ. As long as you believe the python's lies of limitation by thinking, "This is what I've always been, this is where I've always been, and this is all I can ever do," you'll never give the enemy a nightmare.

Are you finished with worry? Are you done with fear? Are you through with defeat, with disease, with lack? You have victory in Jesus's name. Now act like it!

God does not want sickness, disease, and fear running in and out of your life at the devil's whim. We have all power in the name of Jesus. Release that authority. Walk in new dominion. Walk in praise. You have a broken vessel, but you also have a trumpet. Out of your brokenness, pick up a trumpet and sound forth a high praise.

IF NOT FOR PRAISE

In 2 Kings, chapter 3, we find the story of two kings—Jehoram, king of Israel, and Jehoshaphat, king of Judah—who joined forces to defeat the king of Moab. Unfortunately the two kings found themselves in big trouble even before the battle began: they miscalculated the amount of water they needed for the journey.

When they realized their predicament, they thought the Lord had sentenced them to death. Finally Jehoshaphat decided to seek the counsel of the Lord and asked for the prophet of the Lord. They found out that Elisha was nearby, so they sought him out.

Elisha had a double portion of Elijah's anointing. He left everything to follow the call of God. Elisha had miracle power. I can just imagine Elisha sitting at home as the king of Israel and the king of Judah approach with the king of Edom, whose land they were crossing.

Elisha got a little mad. You could even say he got a touch of righteous indignation about the situation. Knowing the sins of Jehoram, Elisha told him to go consult the idol-serving prophets of his mother and father, Ahab and Jezebel.

Concerned that the Lord had given the victory to the enemy, Jehoram pleaded further. Finally Elisha responded, "As the LORD of hosts lives, before whom I stand, surely *were it not that I regard the presence of Jehoshaphat king of Judah*, I would not look at you, nor see you. But now bring me a musician" (vv. 14–15, emphasis added).

Elisha wasn't going to seek the Lord on behalf of a sinning king who had no fear or love of God in his heart. Jehoshaphat was a different story, however. He was the king of Judah, and the name Judah means *Jehovah be praised.* Jehoram may not have done anything right up to this point, except for bringing Jehoshaphat.

Elisha called for some praise music. He needed to invite the presence of the Lord into the situation. As the musician played, the Word of the Lord came to Elisha.

> "Make this valley full of ditches." For thus says the LORD: "You shall not see wind, nor shall you see rain; yet that valley shall be filled with water, so that you, your cattle, and your animals may drink." And this is a simple matter in the sight of the LORD; He will also deliver the Moabites into your hand.
>
> —2 KINGS 3:16–18

Elisha clearly says in verse 14, "If it had not been for praise in this room, I would not even look at you. I would not even listen to you. I would not even give you the time of day. If it were not for the presence of praise in this room, I would just walk out and leave you on your own to get out of this mess."

This situation was bearing down on the kings like a python increasing its pressure. The thing that broke the grip was *praise*. Elisha was saying that when you get in trouble, it takes praise to deliver you. Nothing else would have gotten Jehoram out of this situation.

What situation has you cornered? What dry place are you in right now? Do not let the python grip you so that you cannot praise your way out of it. Break through the grip with the power of praise—even if you don't feel like it, even if it is not a convenient time. With the presence of praise in the room, your revelation can overcome your situation!

I believe there are many lost souls who would still be bound up and held hostage by the devil if it had not been for praise. I believe there are a lot of sicknesses that would still be on people if it had not been for praise. I believe a lot of people would still be held by the throes of depression or addiction if it had not been for praise. Here are a few more things to remember about praise:

1. Praise is a weapon. Some things will not break loose until you shout a good "Hallelujah." Praise is a weapon. It brings victory. It brings deliverance. It helps to make a way where there is no way.

2. Praise activates the spirit world. Rock groups understand that music activates the spirit world, and demons are activated by demonic music. We need to realize that singing praise to God also activates angels, which are called "ministering spirits" (Heb. 1:14).

3. Praise confounds the enemy and releases the power of God.

4. Praise is a lifestyle. Praise is something you do every day. Praise is something with which you fill your mind all week long. You have to live a life of praise if you want to loose the deadly grip of the python.

5. Praise is often simply recounting the faithfulness and greatness of God in times past. We frequently see David and other Old Testament writers reminding the people of God to remember His faithful, wondrous acts.

6. Praise frees others too. When we begin to praise God in spirit and in truth, other people are listening and may be blessed. When Paul and Silas praised and the earthquake brought deliverance,

"everyone's chains were loosed" (Acts 16:26).
When you praise the Lord in your house, you
create an atmosphere where deliverance can
come to everybody around you.

7. Praise must be wholehearted. If you want to get
   a release of God's power in your life, you can't
   be halfhearted about your commitment to God
   by serving Him halfway; you have to go all the
   way. You can't get the blessing if you're only
   half-changed or you only offer Him halfhearted
   praise. The key is to go all the way with God.

No one would deny that Jehoram and Jehoshaphat were
having a tough day. When you think about it, Paul and Silas
were not having their best day either. What made the difference? Praise.

PRAISE HIM IN THE VALLEY

Where do you get the power to prevail in tough times? How
do you have peace in a storm? How do you walk through the
valley of trial and death? One thing I love about David is that
he was not always happy. He suffered some very difficult seasons. He was ridiculed and rejected by his older brothers. King
Saul hunted him and tried repeatedly to kill him. His own
children turned on him in his old age, attempting to take the
throne.

With the presence of praise in the room, your
revelation can overcome your situation!

There are times in Scripture when he is very happy, and there are times when he is extremely low. Like you and me, David was someone who endured the full range of emotions that life can bring. Also like you and me, David had to learn how to be victorious in tough seasons.

Bad times come to good people. You may be in the toughest season of your life right now. We will always be faced with seasons of attack. Pythons get hungry, but you don't have to become prey.

Have you ever taken an amazing vacation that you just couldn't stop raving about when you returned to work? Your coworkers hear you talking about it and become intrigued, wanting to know more. You enthusiastically share every detail with anyone who will listen. Some even say they might book a vacation to the same spot next year. Your praise of the place caused others to want to know more.

The same is true of the Lord. Psalm 76:1 reads, "In Judah God is known; His name is great in Israel." As I mentioned earlier, Judah means *praise*. In praise God is known. When you praise Him, you make Him known to others.

God wants you to understand that you do not come to know Him through mere mental ascension. You come to know Him and all that He can do through worship and praise. He will break the chokehold of the python as you praise Him.

We like to share about our "mountaintop" experiences—those times with God when He heals our hearts, restores our strength, and His love lifts us out of the mud and mire. We don't typically like to talk as much about our "valley" experiences. However, I want to change your opinion about valleys.

In 1 Samuel 17 the Philistine army had come to make war against the army of Israel. The Philistines stood on one mountain and Israel stood on another mountain with a valley between them (v. 3).

Goliath, the champion of the Philistines, stood about nine feet tall and carried a huge shield and a fourteen-foot spear. Every day for forty days he would walk down into that valley to defy God and taunt the army of Israel.

Forty is the number for testing, and Israel was failing the test. Goliath was the first thing they heard in the morning and the last thing they heard at night. Day after day the taunting voice of the enemy and all of his threats would rain down on their ears and erode their confidence.

Those who study mental health will tell you that whatever dominates your mind in the morning and evening will establish what kind of life you are going to have. When you go to bed, you're worried. When you wake up, you're worried. Have you ever had anything just gnaw on your nerves that way? It erodes your confidence just as Goliath's threats did to the Israelite army.

Goliath wanted to occupy the valley, but he did not have ownership of it. The valley belonged to Judah—it belonged to praise! Your valley doesn't belong to fear. It does not belong to stress. It does not belong to intimidation and worry. That valley belongs to praise.

Just as with Gideon, the wrong camp was intimidated. The Israelite army tossed and turned at night with the threats of Goliath echoing in their minds.

The python wants you to give up on praise. He wants to cut off your breath and silence your voice. He threatens you in the morning and tries to ruin your day. You lay your head on your pillow at night, and just as you drift off to sleep, those thoughts of worry and fear fill your head again.

Never give up the valley to the enemy! God says, "That valley belongs to my praise!" Whether you are on the mountaintop or in the valley, you need to praise God! Praise breaks the enemy's python grip in your life.

A young shepherd from Bethlehem named David arrived with food for his brothers in the army. Now David was a worshipper. As a shepherd tending his sheep, David's thoughts had been filled every morning and evening with praise to God.

So when he arrived and heard the defiant rants of the enemy, he couldn't believe the mighty army of Israel was just "taking it" and doing nothing. David went to King Saul and said, "Let me go fight Goliath, because one day I was watching my sheep, and a lion attacked, and I snatched the lamb out of the lion's mouth and slew the lion. Another day a bear attacked, and I killed it with my bare hands. I learned through praise how powerful my God is!"

You know how the story ends, but I want you to understand one thing: David faced Goliath with praise on his lips. He ran toward Goliath with a determination that his enemy would not be victorious in that valley.

You don't have to deny the darkness of the valley when those seasons come along. But you don't have to turn the valley over to the enemy either. Issues are real. Hardships are real. But praise is also real—and it's a very powerful weapon against the enemy.

The real battle was not between David and Goliath. The real battle was about who was going to occupy the valley. You do not have to let fear and worry fill your valley seasons if you choose to worship God in the valley. Your praise has power to break the hold of the python and all the weapons of the enemy.

That praise-filled young man ran toward Goliath, loaded his sling, and let the river rock fly. He made a final, lasting "impression" on Goliath and dropped him where he stood. He cut off Goliath's head, took it back to his tent, and placed it on a pole. He took home the symbol of his victory over the enemy and held it up for all to see.

> The real battle was not between David and Goliath. The real battle was about who was going to occupy the valley.

Your authority doesn't just work on the battlefield. It doesn't just work at church. It works at home as well. It doesn't just sound good while you're reading this book. It works in your life every day if you let it. You need to get such an anointing that you'll carry the headship and authority into your house. You'll establish victory in your home and life.

You'll set up notice as a reminder, "I have authority over every demonic power that tries to come in this home, against this marriage, this family, and these children. I will not give my valleys to the enemy—they will be filled with praise!"

You will know when the python tries to choke out your praise. You find yourself with no desire to lift your hands or lift your voice. You begin filling your eyes and ears with things of this world more than with the Word of God or music that honors Him.

It is time to stop giving in to the chokehold of the enemy. Stop letting him coil around you and have his way. It is time to take the authority that Jesus gave you and put hell on notice. Tell that python, "You're not going to get one of my children, you're not going to wreck my marriage, you're not going to get my finances because I have authority through the blood and through the name of Jesus—and I will praise Him for it!"

Worship and praise—even when broken, even in the valley—make God known and destroy the python grip of the enemy. Next we'll discover the power of the Holy Spirit's presence as an amazing weapon to defeat this deadly predator.

fourteen

THE ARMOR OF GOD

CHRIST SAID, "I have given you authority to trample on snakes and scorpions and to overcome all the power of the enemy; nothing will harm you. However, do not rejoice that the spirits submit to you, but rejoice that your names are written in heaven" (Luke 10:19–20, NIV). This is a promise given by the Lord, and it needs to be grasped by everyone reading this book. When coming against spiritual forces, you must fight against spiritual weapons of the enemy. You must be strong in the Lord.

Put on the whole armor of God, that you may be able to stand against the wiles of the devil. For we do not wrestle against flesh and blood, but against principalities, against powers, against the rulers of the darkness of this age, against spiritual hosts of wickedness in the heavenly places. Therefore take up the whole armor of God that you may be able to withstand in the evil day, and having done all, to stand. Stand therefore, having girded your waist with truth, having put on the breastplate of righteousness, and having shod your feet with the preparation of the gospel of peace; above all, taking the shield of faith with which you will be able to quench all the fiery darts of the wicked one. And take the helmet of salvation, and the sword of the

Spirit, which is the word of God; praying always with all prayer and supplication in the Spirit, being watchful to this end with all perseverance and supplication for all the saints.

—EPHESIANS 6:11–18

To win against the enemy, you must dress for success. Let's take a look at the armor we've been given for spiritual battles. When Paul was in prison, he was primarily guarded by Roman soldiers for several months. He must have had a good chance to examine all of the soldiers' armor up close. In Ephesians 6:14 Paul said, "Stand firm then, with the belt of truth buckled around your waist" (NIV).

THE BELT OF TRUTH

In the Roman armor of Paul's day, the belt, which went around the soldier's waist, was one of the most important pieces of equipment because everything else the soldier needed in battle was fastened to his belt. If the belt wasn't in place, nothing else was secure.

Paul tells us that a Christian's first foundational piece of armor is the belt of truth. If the belt is not secure, then the rest of the armor will fall. If we aren't grounded in truth, we will surely fall. How do we know that we are grounded in truth? We must know the Scriptures by studying the Word of God (the belt of truth).

THE BREASTPLATE OF RIGHTEOUSNESS

The second piece of armor is the breastplate. In Roman armor the breastplate was made of bronze and usually covered with the tough hide of an animal skin. It protected the most vital area of the body, the heart. Proverbs 4:23 says, "Keep thy heart with all diligence; for out of it are the issues of life" (KJV).

Guarding our hearts has to do with understanding the righteousness of God. "For God made Christ, who never sinned, to be the offering for our sin, so that we could be made right with God through Christ" (2 Cor. 5:21, NLT). The breastplate of his righteousness is a reference to the fact that Satan will attack you and accuse you constantly. You must rely on Christ's righteousness.

Satan loves to come and remind you that you have failed God, but if you have the breastplate of His righteousness, you can say, "It's not my righteousness or works that makes God use me or love me; it's the righteousness that has been given to me through Jesus Christ. Therefore I am righteous in God's sight."

THE SHOES OF PEACE

It says in Ephesians 6:15, "And having shod your feet with the preparation of the gospel of peace." Anyone who has ever fought in any kind of hand-to-hand combat knows that sure footing is most important. Muhammad Ali, perhaps the greatest boxer of all time, had a famous saying: "I float like a butterfly and sting like a bee." Floating like a butterfly was a reference to his footwork. Any boxer knows that if they lose their footing, it is only a matter of time before they are defeated.

In fighting with swords, as they did in the time of the Roman legions, losing your footing could mean death, so footgear was very important. In fighting face-to-face combat, their feet had to be planted solid.

In the Christian life we need solid footing. If we are going to walk the walk of faith and resist Satan, we must have our feet shod with the gospel of peace. If we do not learn to depend on God for the promises of peace, then we will not have the sure footing to be able to stand against the blows of Satan. He will knock us off balance and have us on the ground before we know it.

Satan uses worry, anxiety, and fear to keep us off balance, but when Paul said a Christian's feet should be shod with the gospel of peace, he was talking about combatting worry and fear with the promises of God.

Are you afraid? Claim this promise: "Do not fear, for I am with you. Do not anxiously look about you, for I am your God. I will strengthen you, surely I will help you. Surely I will uphold you with My righteous right hand" (Isa. 41:10, NAS).

If you are worried about bills stacking up, the pressures of business, or your children, or if your marriage is mounting with problems, look to the promises of God and claim them. Philippians 4:6 says, "Do not be anxious about anything, but in everything, by prayer and petition, with thanksgiving, present your requests to God" (NIV).

When you get up in the morning, make sure you put on the whole armor of God. Ask yourself, "Do I have the belt of truth? Have I read the Word today? Do I have the breastplate of righteousness? I'm not going to slip into a performance relationship with God; I'm going to put on the breastplate of righteousness. Am I wearing shoes that cover me with the peace of God no matter what storms I face?"

THE SHIELD OF FAITH

The next piece of armor is the shield of faith. Ephesians 6:16 says, "In all circumstances take up the shield of faith, with which you can extinguish all the flaming darts of the evil one" (ESV).

The Roman soldier's shield was about two feet wide and four feet long. He used it to ward off the blows of the enemy, and he also hid behind it when the enemy archers would release a volley of arrows. Roman soldiers could kneel down on the ground and erect a wall of shields around them to block out flaming missiles. If you saw the movie *300*, you saw an accurate depiction of this.

Satan is always firing his hot arrows at us. He is always trying to get inside of us with guilt or some accusation, but if you have the shield of faith protecting you, Christ is more than able to give you the peace and protection you need.

THE HELMET OF SALVATION

The purpose of a Roman soldier's helmet, just like any soldier's helmet, was, of course, to protect the head, another area that needed to be guarded from a fatal blow. The parallel in our spiritual armor is that the helmet protects our heads, or our thought life.

Too many Christians are tormented in their thought life. They believe they have committed some terrible sin, and the enemy comes in and whispers, "I know what you did. It's unpardonable. God won't forgive you." He tries to keep you on a guilt trip.

Putting on the helmet of salvation is knowing that your salvation is absolutely secure and complete. Once you believe in Jesus Christ and repent, you are forgiven for your sin. When the enemy's voice tells you that you don't have eternal life or that you're not forgiven, you just don't listen to him because your mind is covered.

Salvation does not depend upon performance. It never has and never will. It depends upon what Christ did for us. If you do not have the helmet or assurance of salvation, you will not have strong faith. Put on your helmet of salvation.

THE SWORD OF THE SPIRIT

Lastly, the sword is an offensive weapon. In biblical times a Roman sword had a blade that was twenty-four inches long, was sharp on both edges, and pointed at the end.

The Word of God is living and sharper than a two-edged sword. When Jesus was tempted in the wilderness in Luke 4, He gave verses of Scripture to Satan to resist his temptations. There is no greater example from whom we can learn than Jesus. He would quote out loud the verses of Scripture each time Satan attacked Him in the wilderness.

I believe this is how we are to resist the devil. Take God's promises, speak the Word of God and the promises of God, and use the Word like a sword. Keep your sword sharp—by studying and knowing the Word—to defeat the enemy.

Satan attacks us on a daily basis. Therefore we need to check our armor daily and make sure it is polished, oiled, and ready for active duty at all times. Don't allow your sword to get rusty by not studying the Word. Keep it sharp. If your breastplate has slipped out of place and you notice you've begun a performance-based relationship with God, you better adjust it. If your helmet of salvation is loose and you aren't certain of your salvation, then go back to God's Word, get in His presence, and put on your helmet of salvation.

A Lion on a Leash

For we wrestle not against flesh and blood, but against principalities, against powers, against the rulers of the darkness of this world, against spiritual wickedness in high places.

—Ephesians 6:12, KJV

Remember that Jesus has already defeated Satan. *The Pilgrim's Progress* is considered by some to be the next best-selling book after the Bible. Many of you may have read it at some point. If you haven't, I encourage you to pick up a copy and read this famous allegory of the Christian life.

If you have read it, you may remember that Christian was approaching a narrow passage as he traveled toward Porter's lodge for the night. In the narrow passage he saw two lions, but he did not know that the lions were chained. He was very afraid and considered turning back, fearing that nothing but death was before him.

But the porter at the lodge, whose name was Watchful, perceived that Christian was about to turn back, so he cried with a loud voice not to fear the lions because they were chained and could do him no harm. Christian then cautiously walked into the narrow passage, trembling with fear. He heard the lions roar, he felt their hot breath on his flesh, but they did him no harm because they were indeed on the chain. Christian then clapped his hands for joy and went on through the narrow passage and arrived safely on the other side.

I have good news for you about the devil: Satan is a lion on a leash! The devil has power, but his power is limited. He appears often as a roaring lion, but remember this lion is on a leash.

The Bible says, "Resist the devil and he will flee from you," (James 4:7). In his book *Satan: His Personality, Power, and Overthrow*, E. M. Bounds said, "Resist means to set one's self against, to withstand. Yield him nothing at any point, but oppose him at every point. Be always against him, belonging ever to the party of opposition....Firmness, decision, and opposition, these the devil cannot stand."[1]

The greatest fear of demons is the blood of Jesus Christ. The application of the shed blood of Jesus Christ spilled on the cross provides our protection and our victory. We overcome him "by the blood of the Lamb and by the word of [our] testimony" (Rev. 12:11). The devil cannot cross the bloodline. A heart sprinkled with the blood of Jesus Christ is holy ground upon which the devil dares not tread.

Put on the full armor of God daily, plead the blood of Jesus over your life, and you will be victorious in spiritual battles. Read on to discover how to cancel the devil's assignments.

fifteen

CANCEL THE DEVIL'S ASSIGNMENT

A PYTHON MIGHT SEEM harmless if you look at one in a cage at the zoo. You might even watch an animal trainer handle one and think, "Hey, maybe they aren't that dangerous." But make no mistake; a python is a killer. And our spiritual adversary the python is just as deadly. He has an evil agenda, a demonic destiny. He has an assignment from hell to sneak upon us, wrap around us, and choke out our very breath.

But I have good news. The Word declares that Jesus is master of the underworld. He is master of demon powers and unclean spirits. In Philippians 2:9–11 Paul tells us that God has highly exalted Jesus and given Him a name that is above every name, that at the name of Jesus every knee must bow, in heaven and on earth and in the underworld. We see this power displayed in the life of Jesus when we read the fifth chapter of the Gospel of Mark.

Don't Settle Too Far From God's Presence

In Mark 5 the very first thing we learn is that Jesus went to the land of the Gadarenes. Now you need to understand the history of the land of the Gadarenes. I have been to this place. I have seen it. The Gadarene territory that it's referring to is on the east side of the Sea of Galilee and the Jordan River.

The Gadarenes were people whose history went back to the twelve tribes of Israel; they were descendants of the tribe of Gad. You may remember that when Joshua led the children of Israel across the Jordan River into the Promised Land, the tribe of Gad, along with Reuben and half of Manasseh, did not cross over with them. Before Moses died, they got his permission to establish cities and settle permanently along the east side of the river as long as their men helped the Israelites conquer the land when they first crossed over.

I've often marveled that they would give up their inheritance so easily. They judged that the land on the east side of the river was good for livestock, and they wanted to keep their children protected from the Canaanites on the other side of the Jordan. So they struck up a compromise.

To me, they represent what I call "borderline Christians." They decided to trust what they could see with their own eyes rather than trusting God to lead them into unknown territory. They said, "We've come this far, and this is all the farther we're going to follow You, God." They weren't even remotely interested in going and possessing everything God said they could have. They camped out on the borderline while the rest of God's people followed Him into their destiny.

The people of Gad remained on the border as God's presence moved farther and farther away. By the time the ark of the covenant resided in Jerusalem, they were one of the tribes farthest away from the presence of God. (As I previously wrote in this book, the ark of the covenant was the "throne zone," the place where the presence of God resided. When the Israelites crossed the Jordan and took the Promised Land, they carried the ark of God's presence out before them.)

Some of you are like the Gadarenes. You got saved, you

reached the very edge of God's promise, but then you set up camp, made some compromises, and stayed right there on the border. You've been in that same spot for years. You've settled far away from the presence of God. You've settled for what you can see with your own eyes. You've decided it's better to trust your own wisdom and plans for your life instead of trusting God to take you through. You've made your camp on the borderline, settled for compromise, and don't even realize how far from His presence you are.

Too many Christians today worship God from afar. We give Him superficial worship from a distance. We go to church on Sunday morning and barely raise our hands, and when it's all over, we leave God at the back door and go do whatever we want to do the rest of the week.

You want to know why people don't want to come close into the place of worship? Because you can't get close to the presence of God and live like you want to live and do what you want to do. Because when you really get close to the presence of God, you begin to act like He acts and live like He lives. You begin to take on His nature, His character, and His appetites.

Instead we develop a way of avoiding intimacy with God. We have a form of godliness, but we deny its power. We have these little yuppie, high-tech churches now. We just come in and do a little this and do a little that and then go live any way we want to.

But I'm writing this to tell you that you can't keep doing what you want to and get close to God at the same time. You can't set up camp on the borderline and never follow Him into the deeper things He has for you. There comes a point when you have to walk it and live it, or you're simply not in relationship with Him.

Now the Bible says that Jesus included the land of the Gadarenes in His itinerary. I don't believe He was going there just to deliver a demon-possessed man, but I believe He had a historical account to settle in that city because these people had gotten so far from the presence of God that they were raising pigs. Whoever heard of anything so ridiculous? Jews raising pigs!

> We have these little yuppie, high-tech churches now. We just come in and do a little this and do a little that and then go live any way we want to.

Under Moses not only were they forbidden to eat pigs, but also God had forbidden them to even touch them. Pigs were considered filthy and unclean. But the Gadarenes had chosen to live so far from the presence of God that they forgot how He told them to live.

It's amazing what you'll get involved in when you get away from God's presence. That borderline territory had tempted them to settle there with its ideal conditions for livestock. Instead of looking to God as their source, they were looking all around them and taking matters into their own hands, trusting their own decisions. Next thing you know, they were raising pigs and making their living off of pigs. The very thing that God said had no place, the thing that represented uncleanness, was now one of the main sources of their livelihood.

So I believe Jesus was on His way to clean them up. He steps off the boat, and a man was waiting to greet Him. This man, the Bible says, was possessed with demon spirits. I see this man as a representative of the Gadarenes. In other words, he was a reflection of what that people had become because they were so far from the presence of God.

I want you to understand that when you as an individual or we as a church or nation pull away from the presence of God, demons start taking over. Intense demonic activity begins to come into our lives, our churches, and our nation when we draw back from the presence of God and the place of worship.

ONCE A SNAKE, ALWAYS A SNAKE

The Bible says that this man was living among the tombs and walking day and night in the tombs. In other words, this man liked to hang around dead things. He consorted with the dead. He probably liked to go to séances. I bet he liked to try to talk to relatives and play with dead things. It reminds me of people in our time who like to try to find out who or what they were in their "past life" or people who consult mediums to try and communicate with loved ones who have died.

We live in a society that has a fascination with the dead and the occult. We call psychic hotlines and watch *Celebrity Ghost Stories* on TV. Our teenagers entertain themselves with movies and books about vampires like *Twilight* and with TV shows about zombies like *The Walking Dead*. They get into that.

You want to know what's happening? Just as the people of Gad started letting the pigs into their lives, we've allowed the snakes into ours. We've given the python access through TV and the Internet. Our kids are downloading his music and listening to it 24/7. We think, "Oh, it's not that bad. This one episode has someone in it that I like. It won't hurt me to watch it." We befriend the python and get more and more comfortable with sin in our lives. Then we wonder why our kids don't want to listen when we try to talk about the things of God.

It reminds me of the old story about a man who found a wounded snake on the road, and, having compassion, he took it home and nursed it back to health. After spending so much time with the snake, he didn't feel any danger when he was around it. In fact, he had grown quite fond of it and practically considered it a pet.

Then one day as he was feeding the snake, it bit him on the hand, and its poisonous venom quickly spread throughout his body. As he lay there dying, he looked at the snake with complete disbelief in his eyes. "I took such good care of you, I fed you, and kept you safe. How could you bite me?"

Without the slightest bit of remorse the snake sneered as it hissed in reply. "S-s-s-silly man. *You knew I was a snake when you took me in.*"

What snakes have you given safe harbor in your home? What sins have you convinced yourself are harmless, making them your pets while ignoring their deadly nature? What pigs have you let into the parlor? My friend, they might seem harmless at first, but they'll lead to your destruction. Sin is fun for a season, but in the end it leads to death.

If you know something is a sin, don't pick it up. Don't open the door and let it slither into your home. Don't let your children play with it. Don't feed it. It will bite you, it will squeeze the life out of you, and it is deadly.

The Bible says that this demon-possessed man was uncontrollable. He terrorized the people. He had a violent spirit. It was a spirit of rage, a spirit of homicide, a spirit of murder.

We see teenagers gang banging and killing one another just to get in a gang. Men beat their wives black and blue—and it's in the church too. I've seen women coming to church with black eyes because a punk man beat them up. Pedophiles prey on children, and innocent young lives are snatched up into human trafficking every day. People go on a shooting rampage in theaters and schools full of innocent victims. They set off bombs at the Boston Marathon. It's a spirit of murder, a spirit of violence, and it's growing across our nation.

The Bible says this man was bound with chains, but he could not be restrained. I tell you these demons are real! And you don't just wiggle your nose like Samantha on the old show *Bewitched* to make them go away. It doesn't work that way. He's a real devil, but thank God we have this confidence that *greater* is He who is in me than he who is in this world! Praise God for victory over the devil!

When Jesus stepped out of that boat, the Bible says the demons saw Him from afar. They weren't even close, but they recognized Him. They saw Him from afar and became terror-stricken.

Demons ought to get uncomfortable when a child of God walks into the room. Demons ought to get upset when a man or woman full of the Holy Ghost walks onto their territory. Some of you wonder why you get attacked so much. You just go into a store, minding your own business, paying for some gas, and some guy turns around and says, "Blankity, blank, blank, blank!"

Don't you understand what that is? That's the Holy Spirit in you upsetting the unclean spirits all around you. Take it as a compliment. I used to get down about it. I used to get down because it seemed like everywhere I went, people got upset with me. But now I realize that the Holy Ghost is doing His thing. He's on a terrorizing mission to mess up the devil.

Now, back in Mark we see that Jesus said, "What is your name?" The demons said, "My name is Legion, for we are many" (Mark 5:9). *Legion* is a military word that was used to describe a Roman unit of soldiers that would contain a minimum of six thousand to ten thousand soldiers.

And the next thing those demons say is, "We know you're going to throw us out. But please give us a place to go." I love that!

You see, one thing you need to understand about demons is that when they come into the presence of Jesus, they don't do what they want to do anymore. They don't go where they want to go. When a demon gets in the presence of Jesus, he has to ask permission. He has to go according to Jesus's plan then. Jesus's will and purpose override the will of the demon.

And the Bible says the demons came out of the man and went into a large herd of pigs. The pigs went crazy and jumped off a cliff into the sea.

CANCEL THE ENEMY'S ASSIGNMENT

Now those Gadarene people were making their living off those pigs, and they got upset. So they came to see the evidence of what had taken place, and this man was sitting at the feet of Jesus. Now note, first of all, he was sitting. Before he had been uncontrollable; they couldn't even chain him with chains. But now that he has encountered Jesus, he's sitting. He's in control.

I tell you right now as you read this book, that if you'll get into the presence of Jesus, He'll give you control over things you don't have control over. If you'll encounter the presence of Jesus, He'll put you in your right mind and give you control over yourself so you quit doing things that degrade you, put you down, and make you feel like dirt.

But the Gadarenes got so upset that they said, "We don't like this. We didn't want You to kill our pigs. We want You to leave!" They were so far from the presence of God that when they couldn't get to God, Jesus came to them. Before their sins killed them, He killed their pigs. Yet they couldn't see it this way.

I believe the Lord showed me something about this that I want to share with you now. Some of you have some pigs, and you're saying, "I want my pigs; leave my pigs alone." That's what those people did. You can't have Him as Lord and keep your pigs. You can't be alive in Christ if you're dying from the python's death grip.

> One thing you need to understand about demons is that when they come into the presence of Jesus, they don't do what they want to do anymore. They have to ask permission.

I believe the Lord says, "Come into My presence. Come close. Don't sit on the bank of the Jordan somewhere. Don't live in compromise on the borderline. Don't straddle the fence. Come on into the holy of holies and encounter My presence."

I believe our nation is a reflection of a compromised lifestyle that is far from the presence of God, and because of it we have set in motion intense demonic activity. But if our nation will come back into the presence of God and let Him kill our pigs— kill our idols, our lust, our rebellion, and all of the sin that is separating us from Him—then I believe God will cancel the devil's assignment.

I believe those of you struggling with the grip of the python need to understand that God says, "You may feel like you've been far from Me, but I'm coming to you. What I did for the Gadarene man, I can do for you. You've let the python in, and he has you gasping for air, but I can set you free. I can cancel the devil's assignment over your life."

And the Lord says, "If you will come close and let Me get all of these unclean things out of your life, then you can speak to demon powers and cancel the assignment of the devil over your life!"

Cancel the devil's assignment over your life! Cancel the devil's assignment over your family's lives! Every day when your spouse and children wake up, there are demons that have an assignment for them. Cancel the devil's assignment off your children. Cancel the devil's assignment off your spouse. The devil wants to hurt him or her. The python wants to choke the life out of him or her. Cancel his assignment in the name of Jesus!

Cancel the devil's assignment over your church. He's plotting out there somewhere. But if you have God's presence living in you, you have the power to cancel the devil's assignment over your life.

Before you get in your car, cancel the devil's assignment. Before you get on an airplane and fly anywhere, cancel his assignment. Wherever you go, cancel the devil's assignment in that place.

In every area of your life—in your finances he has an assignment to bring poverty; in your health he has an assignment to bring disease. You know what you need to do: cancel the devil's assignment in the name of Jesus Christ!

Don't let this chapter give you a spirit of fear. You don't have to go around worrying if you'll cancel the devil's assignment.

You don't have to take life as it comes if you'll cancel the devil's assignment.

Some of you have been worrying about his assignment. You've been talking about his assignment. You've paced the floor over his assignment. You know he has something brewing. But just cancel the devil's assignment.

Speak the power of God's Word, and cancel the devil's assignment. "Our weapons...are not carnal, but mighty through God to the pulling down of strongholds" (2 Cor. 10:4, KJV). What you bind or cancel on earth will be canceled in heaven (Matt 18:18). You can cancel the devil's assignment, and before you move on to the last chapter about starting a "chain reaction," remember this:

There is more power in the name of Jesus than all the demons in hell!

sixteen

START A "CHAIN REACTION"

W E'VE ALL BEEN amazed by death-defying feats that magicians and stunt artists perform. Many times they will wrap themselves in chains before they are dropped into a tank of water, pushing themselves to the very edge of dying as they struggle to free themselves before they run out of air. There's something about seeing someone wrapped in chains that we all identify with, and we all want to see them get free.

A chain is joined links of metal that symbolize captivity in our minds. When we see someone in chains, it instigates a reaction. A fight arises inside of us that starts pulling for that person to get free from those chains.

If we allow him, our enemy the python will wrap himself around us just like a chain and absolutely stop us from going forward and being free. Python has many ways of imposing his invisible chains on us—invisible chains that minimize our mobility, invisible chains that stop and hinder our progression in life.

If we are the prey of the python, those chains can take on many forms, and they are very real. They can be drugs. They can be low self-esteem. It can be the chain of fear or depression that wraps itself around us when bad news comes. I think of the chain of eating disorders that many young teenage girls and women wrestle with. The chains may represent a website, a pornography addiction. The chain of drugs and alcoholism. The chain of shame of a past abuse or a past failure. Layer after layer the enemy coils around you and chains you and tries to hold you captive and hinder you from moving forward.

When the enemy tries to throw chains around you to hinder you, you have to have a reaction to those chains. You have to have a "chain reaction." We normally think of a chain reaction being like a car wreck, and when something happens to one person, there is a reaction again and again as one car slams into the back of another.

That's not the kind of "chain reaction" I'm talking about. The "chain reaction" I'm talking about is the reaction you need to have whenever the python comes and tries to bind you. You see, a lot of people get wrapped up in things, and they can't get free—not because God can't set them free, but because they don't have the proper reaction to those chains.

You don't have enough in you that reacts and says, "I refuse the chain of fear. I refuse the chain of worry. I refuse the chain of depression. I will not wear it. I will not allow it to take hold of me." But if you want to be free, you have to react to whatever is holding you back.

Jesus will help you, but you have to have a "chain reaction" or that python will wrap itself around you. It will squeeze the joy out of you. It will defeat you, and you'll go around discouraged, depressed, hopeless, and ineffective for the kingdom of God.

Praise and prayer are what start the "chain reaction" against the things that bind and enslave you. A lot of people don't understand why I praise the Lord as I do—with lifted hands and shouts of praise. At times I get exuberant about my praise.

Why is that? It's a "chain reaction" to the things that used to be on me that are not on me anymore. And that's why I lift my hands. That's why I sing. That's why I shout. That's why I praise God. It's a chain reaction.

> A lot of people get wrapped up in things and they can't get free—not because God can't set them free, but because they don't have the proper reaction to those chains.

Sometimes you need to have a chain reaction. Sometimes you need to say, "I want to feel free again. I don't have to be chained up to worry and all stressed out about the situation and the pressure I'm under. I refuse these chains. I'm gonna have a chain reaction." Your chain reaction needs to be, "I'll praise God at all times. His praise will continually be in my mouth."

Sometimes you have to say, "I'm tired of being wrapped up in depression. I'm tired of being wrapped up in fear. I'm tired of being wrapped up in joylessness and anxiety. I'm tired of it, and I'm gonna have a chain reaction."

THE ORIGINAL "JAILHOUSE ROCK"

Perhaps there's no greater story of jailbreak than the story of Paul and Silas I've written about throughout this book. There's a reason I chose that story to illustrate the power of breaking loose from the python's deadly grip.

The Bible says that Paul and Silas had been beaten, falsely accused, stripped, put in chains, and thrown into prison. But the most important part of that story in Acts 16 is not how unjustly Paul and Silas were treated. The most important part of that story is not how wrong it was for them to be beaten and how bad the trial was that they went through. All of us go through things that are unfair.

Even with God it doesn't always seem fair the way things turn out. It seems like He blesses some people, and other people go through things that are so severe. And it seems unjust. Then there are those times when it feels like you've been beaten by the circumstances of life and beaten by trials and tribulations. We can all identify with that.

The most important part of the story is in their reaction to what happened to them. When they were chained, they had a reaction that was not normal. When life beats you down and trials beat you down, and when you're treated unjustly, you have to choose the proper reaction to those chains.

You can let that problem wrap itself around you and squeeze the joy out of you until you lose your peace and go into worry, fear, and depression. You can either let it wrap like a python until you worry yourself sick about your children and your family, or you can have a chain reaction.

Paul and Silas were chained up, beaten up, messed up, and treated unfairly. But at midnight they prayed and sang praises unto God. That's the proper "chain reaction." I don't know what you're going through, but I'm writing to tell you what your proper reaction is: "I refuse to be the prey of the python. I refuse to let the enemy turn these problems into chains that bind me. I will praise the Lord in my midnight hour."

I don't care what you're going through. I don't care how bad it is. Have a chain reaction. Refuse those chains by praising the Lord. It's not that your chains aren't real, but it's your *reaction* to the problems of life that releases God.

When you feel depression trying to come on you, or worry or fear, here's your chain reaction: "Praise the Lord! God is good. God is on the throne. I will not fear, for He is with me." You'll feel the chain of worry popping, the chain of fear breaking apart, and the chain of depression lifting when you begin to have a chain reaction.

> Even with God it doesn't always seem fair the way things turn out. It seems like He blesses some people, and other people go through things that are so severe.

The Bible says the other prisoners heard them. Sometimes you're not praising God for yourself. Sometimes you're not worshipping and making noise for yourself. Sometimes people around you are stressed out, on the verge of giving up, addicted, and bound up. And all it takes is for the people of God to begin to praise the Lord, and the prisoners hear our praise.

The Bible says that when the power and presence of God hit that jailhouse, it rocked; it experienced an earthquake. The building was rocked to its foundation, everyone's shackles were loosed, and every prison door was opened. Now that's what I call a jailhouse rock!

Everyone in that prison was set free by the chain reaction of Paul and Silas. You may have family members who are messed up, but God says, "If you have the right reaction and refuse the chains, I'll set other captives free." There'll be a chain reaction.

SPIRITUAL STOCKHOLM SYNDROME

The human psyche is fascinating because truly one has to choose to be free. There's an interesting phenomenon that occurs in people who have been abducted, raped, abused, and kidnapped called Stockholm syndrome. It's named for a study that was done in Stockholm, Sweden, in 1973 that identified an emotional attachment the victims of crimes develop for their captors. It's as if they develop sympathy for the status that they've been in, and they've been in it so long that they begin to accept the defeat. They begin to accept the bondage.

There are a lot of people who have spiritual Stockholm syndrome. They have lived so long and been so defeated so long, so depressed so long, and so addicted so long that they actually have become sympathetic with that status.

If you're in this state, you might think things such as, "I have a right to be depressed. I have a right to be fearful. I have a right to be afraid. Nothing good has happened in my life." You have become so accustomed to failure, so accustomed to losing, so accustomed to being bound and defeated and depressed that you actually have a sense of loyalty to that status.

If spiritual Stockholm syndrome gets hold of you, you'll actually believe what your captor, the devil, has told you about yourself more than you believe the truth. That's why a young girl can look in the mirror and hate what she sees. Even though she's thin, a voice is telling her, "You're fat, you're ugly." That chain of anorexia gets on her, and after a while she actually becomes sympathetic to the captivity that she's in.

That's what happens to people. You begin to wear the chains that the enemy puts on you, and you stay depressed, doubtful, discouraged, and hopeless. And you stay that way day after day, week after week. You have to have a chain reaction that says, "I refuse these chains. These chains do not belong on a child of God. Where the spirit of the Lord is, there is freedom—not worry, not depression, not defeat, not anxiety about my children or my family. I'm gonna have a chain reaction and refuse those chains."

When you have the proper chain reaction, it begins to affect others in your family. God says, "If I can get one to have a chain reaction, there will be a chain reaction in that whole family."

RISE AND SHINE!

We read in Acts 12 that Peter was in prison, and they chained his hands and his feet. But there are a few keys I want you to notice: first, it says *a light shone into his prison.* That's what I'm doing right now. I'm writing these words to deliver a message from God, and a light is shining into people's prisons of fear where they're chained with depression, addiction, bondages, lies, and shame. You've been chained to it. But the light of God's Word is shining.

> If spiritual Stockholm syndrome gets hold of you, you'll actually believe what your captor, the devil, has told you about yourself more than you believe the truth.

The next thing Peter knew, the angel said, "Come on, let's get out of here." And Scripture says that *when he got up, his chains fell off.* The second key is that sometimes you have to take a stand. You need to arm yourself with your spiritual armor (Eph. 6) and stand against the python for your chains to fall off.

Here's the next key: Peter had to follow his angel out of that prison. God will burst open with revelation and with light the potential for you to be free. If you're bound by addiction, if you're bound by drugs or alcohol or depression, God has burst open your prison. The light is shining, but you have to follow where He's leading. You have to do your part. You have to have a chain reaction. You have to say, "I refuse these chains, and I will not be an addict. And when I get free, it's gonna touch my family, it's gonna touch my friends, it's gonna be a chain reaction." It will start with you, but it won't stop with you. God will keep the blessing flowing until your family is saved.

I want to ask you a question that requires a real answer. Do you have some chains in your life? I'm not just writing about addiction to alcohol, drugs, nicotine, and so forth. But I've found the chain that I have to keep having a reaction to or it'll wrap itself around me is worry, fear, discouragement, and depression.

The Bible says in Jeremiah 29:11 that God has good plans for you, plans to give you hope. Anything that is so darkening your mind and your heart that you don't have hope is not the voice of the Holy Spirit. And you have to have a chain reaction to break free. You can be a different person than you were when you started reading this book. You can say, "Whatever happens, God is *with* me, God is *for* me, God is *in* me, and it's gonna be all right."

You may have an addiction. Jesus can set you free, but you have to have a chain reaction. You have to follow the angel. Light has shone into your prison. Now follow the angel. He's going to lead you to freedom.

He's calling you to freedom, and it's not just for you. You are the one in your family whom God's going to use. When they see the change in you, your family members who are bound in the same chains, who are being choked by the python, are going to want what you have. It's a miracle. It can happen for you. It can happen for your family.

I want you to picture any chains that have been wrapped around you. Anything that has been limiting you. Anything that has been holding you back. I believe those chains can be severed. Pray this prayer.

> *Lord Jesus, I surrender my life to You. No more chains. Break every chain in my life that has been holding me back from all that You have for me. Set me free. Give me a brand-new life. I don't want to be chained to the pain of the past. I don't want to be bound up by the python, so I give everything over to You. Wash me, cleanse me, and I'm ready to follow my angel out of bondage into a place of freedom. I receive it, for he whom the Son sets free is free indeed. I receive freedom from* [say whatever you need to break free from right now]. *I am no longer the prey of the python. Lord Jesus, this is my chain reaction.*
>
> *In Jesus's name, amen.*

CONCLUSION

SEVERAL YEARS AGO I read a newspaper article about the pollution problem in the Los Angeles area. The article reported that after commissioning an environmental expert to do an extensive study on what Los Angeles could do about their pollution problem and spending massive amounts of money on this research, the expert called everyone together, including the mayor and city officials, to report his findings. He surprised everyone when he proclaimed that after all his research he had concluded that there was no solution to their pollution problem. Can you imagine that?

But here's what really jumped out at me as I read this story. The newspaper said that after sharing his report and coming to the conclusion that there was no solution, the expert paused and said these words like an afterthought: "What you really need is *a wind from elsewhere* to come and sweep through the city and blow all of this pollution out to sea."

Now, being a preacher, when I read that he said nothing can fix the pollution problem except "a wind from elsewhere," the spiritual parallel was crystal clear to me. Look around at our spiritual condition today. There's pollution, isn't there? You don't have to look very far to find it.

Yet this isn't the first time God's people have become polluted. In Malachi chapter 1 we find that the land was filled with wickedness, idolatry, and sin. The worship had become polluted in the temple. God told the people that their sacrifices were polluted because they were offering animals that were stolen, lame, or sick. He also judged them for the condition of their hearts: they were weary of sacrificing and sneered at the idea of doing it.

Remember, in the Old Testament the sacrifice of an animal would sweep away people's sins for one year so they could live under the favor, help, and protection of God for the next twelve months. But the pollution of sin had become so great that God said, "I won't accept your sacrifices."

The land was polluted with sin, adultery, idolatry, and corruption in the ministry, and God had stopped speaking. It seemed as though there was no solution to the sin problem. When the Book of Malachi closes, God says, "Because of your sins and your hardheartedness, I will smite the earth with a curse."

So between the end of the Old Testament and the beginning of the New Testament, there was a six-hundred-year span. During that entire time God did not speak to man. For six hundred years He refused to speak.

That means that at the beginning of the New Testament there was not a man alive who had had an encounter with God. It was a dark time spiritually. And the pollution of sin would not lift off of the human race.

But then in Acts, chapter 2, the Bible says, "Now when the Day of Pentecost had fully come...suddenly there came a sound from heaven, as a rushing mighty wind" (vv. 1–2). There came *a wind from elsewhere.*

It filled the Upper Room. It filled the church that had become formal and religious and yet had lost the intensity and passion for God. When God breathed that *wind from elsewhere* in Acts 2, verse 1, it began to sweep out all of the pollution, corruption, iniquity, and sin that had built up since the days of Malachi.

Those 120 people in the Upper Room represented generations of people who had been cursing, lying, cheating, and stealing, and when they were hit by the *wind from elsewhere*, it swept the uncleanness out of their life and took it out into a sea of forgetfulness, to be remembered no more.

That's what we need in the church today. That's what America and our cities need. There is no solution for our pollution of sin! We need *a wind from elsewhere!*

You cannot get enough counseling to heal the pollution of sin. I'm not saying counseling doesn't have its place. It certainly does. But sometimes we're guilty of looking to everything and everybody except the One who can get the trash and the filth out of our lives.

The "experts" don't have a solution for your sin pollution! At some point the Holy Spirit has to get hold of your heart and sweep it clean. That *wind from elsewhere* has to blow through and make you a new creation. He has to change your desires, change your thinking, and change your nature! That is the power of the Holy Spirit.

The Holy Spirit has the power to sweep you clean! That *wind from elsewhere* cleanses everything. It can sweep alcohol or sexual immorality out of you forever! There is *a wind from elsewhere* that can blow the pollution of sin away to the sea of forgetfulness, where God will never remember it or hold it against you again.

There is *a wind from elsewhere* that makes us alive. It can enter your life and make a way where there seems to be no way. "'Not by might nor by power, but by My Spirit,' says the LORD of host" (Zech. 4:6).

You don't just need that *wind from elsewhere* one time; the enemy certainly isn't going to give up and go away after you've kicked him out only once. You need the Holy Spirit to come through every once in a while and sweep away your old ways and your old thinking. When you feel that python squeezing the life out of you, that's when you need *a wind from elsewhere* to sweep away your carnality and your lust!

When He comes, He cleanses your heart. He cleanses your spirit. He cleanses your mind from the pollution and the filth of this world. He breaks you free from the python's chokehold and makes you glad you're alive again.

This *wind from elsewhere* will make you fast and pray. It will make you read your Bible. It will make you live right. Sometimes we just can't go any further until we say, "Lord, set me free. Lord, give me liberty again. Lord, send a wind."

Some of you've gone too long without it. It's been too long since you let yourself become broken before God with tears streaming down your face. You don't pray anymore. You don't read the Bible anymore. What you need is *a wind from elsewhere*. It will make you pray! It will make you love God! It will make you wake up in the middle of the night and feel angels in the room.

CAN IT HAPPEN AGAIN TODAY?

In Topeka, Kansas, in 1900, students at Charles Parham's Bethel Bible School began to discuss whether the Holy Spirit could still come like a "mighty rushing wind" and fill people, causing them to "speak with other tongues, as the Spirit gave them utterance" (Acts 2:2, 4). It didn't matter if they were in geometry class or English class, the topic would always turn to this subject.

Finally the hunger became so intense that they declared a fast for the close of 1900 going into the New Year. They agreed to fast and pray for God to fill them with the same Holy Spirit power that they read about in Acts chapter 2. This is exactly what a group of thirty-four students did, and on New Year's Day 1901 suddenly there came *a wind from elsewhere.*

It first hit a young woman who began speaking in Chinese, and soon the *wind from elsewhere* blew on the rest of the group. They spoke in at least twenty-one known languages that were verified by native speakers who turned up at many of the meetings. These events became known as the *Topeka Outpouring.*

But that was just the beginning. In 1905 a former slave named Lucy Farrow spent two months with Charles Parham's family in Topeka. Farrow was leading a small Holiness church in Houston, Texas, and was hungry for an Acts 2 encounter with God. She left a man named William J. Seymour in charge of her Houston flock while she was on her quest to Topeka. The Parham family followed Lucy back to Houston, Texas, where Charles set up a Bible school very similar to Bethel in Topeka.

Seymour, who had been on his own quest for an encounter with the Holy Spirit, attended Parham's Bible school in Houston, and by early 1906 Seymour accepted an invitation to lead a congregation in Los Angeles, California. Although he still had not personally had an experience of speaking in tongues, he was profoundly affected by the teaching of Parham, and upon arriving in Los Angeles, he began to preach about the power of the Holy Spirit and speaking in tongues. When the doors of his congregation's meeting place were padlocked shut, he began to fast and pray, hoping he would soon experience a powerful spiritual encounter. Hours turned into days, and others began to join him in his vigil.

At one such prayer meeting Edward Lee, a janitor at a local bank and attender of Seymour's church, had a powerful vision of Peter and Paul shaking under the power of the Holy Ghost. After he shared this vision with the prayer group, Seymour laid his hands on his friend to pray for him. Lee's legs buckled, and down to the ground he went. Seymour knew something profound had just begun. *A wind from elsewhere* had begun to blow.

Seymour continued to fast and pray and soon relocated his congregation to 312 Azusa Street in Los Angeles. A revival broke out that went on day and night for three and a half years. People came from all over the world, and the modern-day Pentecostal movement was birthed out of that *wind from elsewhere* that started at 312 Azusa Street. Several major denominations with churches around the world are in existence today as a result of Seymour's prevailing prayer and fasting for *a wind from elsewhere.*[1]

So as a preacher who knows all about the Holy Spirit outpouring that began on Azusa Street, it took on a whole different meaning for me when I read the newspaper article about the expert uttering the words to the city officials in Los Angeles, "What you really need is *a wind from elsewhere.*"

I wish I could have been in that meeting when the expert announced this to the mayor of Los Angeles. I would have stood up and said, "Sir, I can take you to a place in Los Angeles where the 'wind' came. And if you can tap into this 'wind,' it will sweep the gangs out of Los Angeles; it will sweep prostitution out. It will clean up Hollywood. It will clean up our nation!"

What America needs is *a wind from elsewhere.* It can clean your city from the gangs, drugs, child abuse, murders, and from all the other sin problems for which there is no earthly solution. As hard as our law enforcement people try—and thank God for them—there is only one thing that can stop the spiritual pollution that is taking place in our nation, our cities, and our schools. We need a fresh *wind from elsewhere* to change us.

Just as the bones in Ezekiel chapter 37 came together, that *wind from elsewhere* can put us back together and stand us on our feet again. The devil may have told you, "You're never going to get on your feet again. This economy has wrecked you, and you're never going to amount to anything." You've been knocked down.

The python whispers his lies and tries to choke out the wind of God in our lives, but the Holy Spirit has all power in heaven and earth. When He starts moving, nothing's impossible! When He starts moving, you can prosper in a famine; you can set records while other people are going under. You can regain everything that was lost, and then some!

Maybe you've been through a divorce, and hell has told you, "You're down for the count, and you'll never get on your feet again." But I've written this book to give you a word from the Lord: There's *a wind from elsewhere* that can get you back on your feet again! I don't care how bad you messed up. I don't care how bad you failed. I'm telling you, when the "wind" comes, He picks you back up; He fills you full of life; He says, "Get on your feet again; I'm not through using you!"

It's time for you to receive *a wind from elsewhere* to sweep away everything that's not like Jesus. It's time to break free from the grip of the python and breathe in deeply of that wind. How long has it been since you had *a wind from elsewhere* filling up your life? Ask God to fill you with the Holy Ghost, and He'll clean up your house, clean up your family, and clean up your attitude.

If you're mad and bitter against anybody, you need *a wind from elsewhere*. It will sweep religion out of you. It will sweep prejudice out of you. It will sweep hate out of you. It will sweep anger and offense out of you.

You don't have an answer for the pollution of your sin. You can't fix you. You need *a wind from elsewhere*. If you do not have a personal relationship with Jesus Christ and you are reading this book, I encourage you right now to confess your sin to Him, ask His forgiveness, and invite Him into your life. That's step one. But I also believe that many people reading this book have been calling themselves Christians for a long time, and yet they desperately need a fresh encounter with God. The python has been choking them for so long they don't even realize they are no longer breathing and the life has gone out of them.

If you're not in too much of a hurry to close this book, you can have an old-fashioned Holy Ghost revival right now. All it takes is for you to hunger and thirst for it and humble yourself. The wind blows where it faces least resistance. That's why the wind blows down alleys so strongly. It can't go through brick walls; it has to find a different direction, so it finds alleys and other open spaces. I've often noticed how much windier it is whenever I'm near a lake or the ocean. Why? Because the atmosphere is wide open there. There are no buildings or walls to resist the wind.

The Holy Spirit is looking for those who are open to *a wind from elsewhere*. If you know right now after reading this book that you need a fresh wind to sweep some stuff out of your life, clean you up, and set you free, I want you to open yourself up and let the wind blow. Begin to ask God for a fresh touch of His Holy Spirit in your life.

It doesn't matter if you're a teenager or a grandparent, whether you own your own business or you are a stay-at-home mom, whether you've been living on the streets or you've been in church for twenty years. Maybe you're a pastor or ministry leader, but that doesn't matter either. If you haven't had a mighty encounter with God in a long time, it's time for *a wind from elsewhere*. What good does it do to hear a lifetime of sermons and read libraries of books if you never encounter His presence?

I know that writing this has stirred something in my spirit, and my hope is that it has also stirred yours. I've prayed for you during the writing of this book, and I want you to know that you don't have to live with depression. You don't have to live with hopelessness. You don't have to live with addiction. You don't have to live a powerless, lukewarm Christian life. You don't have to settle for being the prey of the python. You can be victorious through the power of the Holy Spirit!

Cut off every access point that gives the python a chance to wrap himself around your life. Set aside time daily to breathe in the Word of God and breathe out with prayer and praise to God. This is your spiritual breath, and it is critical for you to live a strong, powerful Christian life. And lastly, open your heart to the Holy Spirit, invite Him in, and breathe His fresh *wind from elsewhere* that will empower you to live the rest of your life on fire for God and passionate about Jesus!

NOTES

CHAPTER 1
A SNAKE IN THE GRASS

1. Bob Janisky, "Creature Feature: Burmese Pythons Prowl the Everglades, and That's Not a Good Thing," National Parks Traveler, May 2, 2009, http://www.nationalparks traveler.com/2009/05/creature-feature-burmese-pythons -prowl-everglades-and-s-not-good-thing (accessed May 6, 2013).

2. Bob Janisky, "Eradicating Everglades Pythons Will be a Formidable Task," National Parks Traveler, July 20, 2009, http://www.nationalparkstraveler.com/2009/07/eradicating -everglades-pythons-will-be-formidable-task (accessed May 6, 2013).

3. Christine Dell'Amore, "Biggest Burmese Python Found in Florida—17.7 Feet, 87 Eggs," NationalGeographic.com, August 14, 2012, http://news.nationalgeographic.com/ news/2012/08/120814-burmese-python-snake-florida-eggs -biggest-science (accessed May 6, 2013).

CHAPTER 4
WHO LET THE SNAKES IN?

1. Duncan Campbell, "Revival in the Hebrides," Revival -Library.org, http://www.revival-library.org/pensketches/ revivals/hebrides.html (accessed May 7, 2013).

CHAPTER 5
GET THE SNAKE EGGS OUT!

1. Rebecca G. Harvey, Matthew L. Brien, Michael S. Cherkiss, et al., "Burmese Pythons in South Florida: Scientific Support for Invasive Species Management," Electronic Data Information Source, University of Florida, Publication #WEC242, http://edis.ifas.ufl.edu/uw286 (accessed May 7, 2013).

2. San Diego Zoo, "Reptiles: Python," http://www.sandiegozoo.org/animalbytes/t-python.html (accessed May 7, 2013).

3. "Internet Pornography Statistics," TopTenReviews.com, http://internet-filter-review.toptenreviews.com/internet-pornography-statistics.html (accessed May 7, 2013).

4. FoxNews.com, "Smoking One Joint Is Equivalent to 20 Cigarettes, Study Says," January 29, 2008, http://www.foxnews.com/story/0,2933,326309,00.html (accessed May 7, 2013).

5. "Pray for Polanski," http://minadream.com/romanpolanski/InterviewThree.htm (accessed May 8, 2013).

CHAPTER 14
THE ARMOR OF GOD

1. E. M. Bounds, *Satan: His Personality, Power, and Overthrow* (N.p.: Fleming H. Revell, 1922), 137. Viewed at Google Books.

CONCLUSION

1. Craig Borlaise, *William Seymour: A Biography* (Lake Mary, FL: Charisma House, 2006), 57–127.

Open the door to a DEEPER, more INTIMATE, more POWERFUL relationship with GOD

New York Times Best Seller

fasting

Opening the door to a deeper, more intimate, more powerful relationship with God

Jentezen Franklin

978-1-59979-258-3 | US $15.99

Jentezen Franklin explains the spiritual power of fasting and offers a deeper understanding of the benefits available to all who participate.

Based on the New York Times Best Seller

fasting JOURNAL

Your personal 21-day guide to a successful fast

Jentezen Franklin

978-1-59979-366-1 | US $14.99

New York Times Best Seller

fasting

Opening the door to a deeper, more intimate, more powerful relationship with God

NOW with DVD!
$19.99

Jentezen Franklin

978-1-61638-198-1 | US $19.99

Based on the New York Times Best Seller

fasting STUDY GUIDE

5-WEEK Interactive Study Resource

Jentezen Franklin

978-1-59379-768-7 | US $9.99

New York Times best-selling author of Fasting

Jentezen Franklin

ALL NEW principles gleaned from twenty years of leading successful fasts worldwide

The fasting EDGE

RECOVER YOUR PASSION
RECAPTURE YOUR DREAM
RESTORE YOUR JOY

978-1-61638-584-2 | US $15.99

New York Times best-selling author of Fasting

Jentezen Franklin

The fasting EDGE JOURNAL

A PERSONAL 21-DAY GUIDE

978-1-61638-850-8 | US $14.99

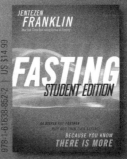

JENTEZEN FRANKLIN
New York Times Best-selling Author of Fasting

FASTING STUDENT EDITION

GO DEEPER AND FURTHER WITH GOD THAN EVER BEFORE
BECAUSE YOU KNOW THERE IS MORE

978-1-61638-852-2 | US $14.99

VISIT YOUR LOCAL BOOKSTORE

www.CharismaHouse.com
www.facebook.com/CharismaHouse

CHARISMA HOUSE

11969

Enjoy these additional messages
from *New York Times* best-selling author

Jentezen Franklin

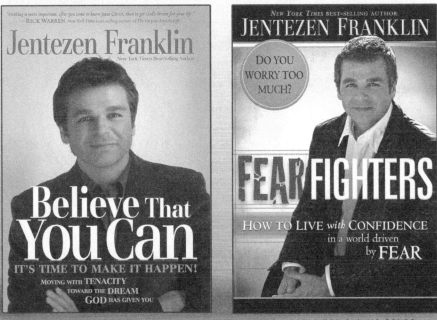

978-1-59979-348-1 | US $21.99   978-1-59979-762-5 | US $21.99

CHARISMA
HOUSE

Visit Your Local Bookstore
Also available for purchase online and as e-books

www.CharismaHouse.com
Facebook.com/CharismaHouse | Twitter.com/charismahouse

11969

FREE NEWSLETTERS
TO HELP EMPOWER YOUR LIFE

Why subscribe today?

☐ **DELIVERED DIRECTLY TO YOU.** All you have to do is open your inbox and read.

☐ **EXCLUSIVE CONTENT.** We cover the news overlooked by the mainstream press.

☐ **STAY CURRENT.** Find the latest court rulings, revivals, and cultural trends.

☐ **UPDATE OTHERS.** Easy to forward to friends and family with the click of your mouse.

CHOOSE THE E-NEWSLETTER THAT INTERESTS YOU MOST:

- Christian news
- Daily devotionals
- Spiritual empowerment
- And much, much more

SIGN UP AT: **http://freenewsletters.charismamag.com**

8178